TV Neighbors: Westport And Weston Television Personalities 1946-2003
© 2011 Thomas A. DeLong. All Rights Reserved.

All illustrations are copyright of their respective owners, and are also reproduced here in the spirit of publicity. Whilst we have made every effort to acknowledge specific credits whenever possible, we apologize for any omissions, and will undertake every effort to make any appropriate changes in future editions of this book if necessary.

Vintage TV sets from the Tony and Susan Eastman collection.

No part of this book may be reproduced in any form or by any means, electronic, mechanical, digital, photocopying or recording, except for the inclusion in a review, without permission in writing from the publisher.

Published in the USA by:
BearManor Media
PO Box 1129
Duncan, Oklahoma 73534-1129
www.bearmanormedia.com

ISBN 978-1-59393-649-5

Printed in the United States of America.
Cover Illustration by Wally Woods.
Book design by Brian Pearce | Red Jacket Press.

TV Neighbors

*Westport and Weston
Television Personalities
1946 - 2003*

THOMAS A. DeLONG

Table of Contents

Preface ix
Introduction xi

FIRST TV OWNER

O.B. Hanson 16

PIONEERS

Victor Keppler 20
Sigmund Spaeth 22
Dorothy Bryce 24
Bill Leonard 26
Win Elliot 28
Eva Le Gallienne 30
John Lodge 32

DRAMA

Bette Davis 36
Joanne Woodward 38
John Malkovich 40
Shirley Knight 42
Dana Andrews 44
Alan Arkin 46
Mia Farrow 48
Tina Louise 50
Carole Shelley 52
David Wayne 54
Christopher Plummer 56
Diana Douglas 58
Bruce Weitz 60
Michael Douglas 62
Frank Lovejoy 64
Mason Adams 66
Mariette Hartley 68
Darren McGavin 70
Pamela Sue Martin 72
Jack Klugman 75
James Naughton 77
David Marshall Grant 78
Michael Hayden 80
Joan Banks 81
Frank Converse 82
June Havoc 84
Paul Newman 86
Patricia Kalember 88
Michael Jai White 90
David Rogers 92
Amanda Rogers 94
Dulcy Rogers 96

COMEDY

Christopher Lloyd 100
Patricia Englund 102
Joan Blondell 104

Barbara Rhoades 106
Madeline Kahn 108
Brett Somers 110
Phyllis Newman 112
Marlo Thomas 114
Martha Raye 116
Mabel Albertson 118
Eva Gabor 120
Imogene Coca 122
Kerri Kenney-Silver 124
Frank Gorshin 126
Kipp Marcus 128
David Groh 130
Alisan Porter 132

SOAPS

Ed Bryce 134
Scott Bryce 136
Kevin Conroy 138
William Prince 140
Larry Haines 142
Mary Stuart 144
Frank Runyeon 146
Martin West 148
Victoria Wyndham 150
Lisa Chapman 152
Haila Stoddard 154
Whit Connor 156
Bobra Suiter 158

MUSIC & DANCE

Cindy Gibb 160
Eartha Kitt 162
James Melton 164
Bambi Lynn & Rod Alexander ... 166
Neil Sedaka 168
Fritz Reiner 170

HOSTS

Don Imus 174
David Susskind 176
Phil Donahue 178
Rod Serling 180
Martha Stewart 182
Sonny Fox 184
Jack Clark 186
Matt Gallant 188

BROADCAST JOURNALISTS

Douglas Edwards 190
Harry Reasoner 192
John MacVane 194
John Siegenthaler 196
Robert Hager 198
Pauline Frederick 200
Eric Burns 202
Dianne Wildman 203
Gordon F. Joseloff 204

SPORTS

Brent Musburger 208
Sal Marchiano 210
Bob Costas 212
Jim Nantz 214
Jim McKay 216
Frank Deford 218

SITCOMS COME TO WESTPORT

I Love Lucy 222
Bewitched 224
My World and Welcome to It 226

Index 229
Bibliography 235
About the Author 236

Dedication

To the best of friends, Denise and Wally Woods, whose dedication and determination made this book possible. Much love, KRCD

Preface

This book grew out of an exhibit, Westport and Weston TV Neighbors, at the Westport, Connecticut, Historical Society. It inaugurated the Society's new Betty and Ralph Sheffer Exhibition Hall in 2003.

I produced that exhibit, skillfully assisted by Wally Woods, Mollie Donovan, Dorothy Bryce and Mindy Mooney. The TV Neighbors Exhibit committee also included Cheryl and Erin Bliss, Howard Munce, Carol Young, Kim Cooper, Gordon Joseloff, Alice Shelton, Nancy Cash and Nancy Roberts. The television performers and other on-camera broadcasters featured in that exhibit, and now in this book, have gained wide fame, while off-screen they became part of everyday life in the Westport and Weston communities where they live or resided at one time.

The biographical text for the majority of these 100 performers does not generally describe their careers beyond 2003, since the exhibit covered the years 1946 to 2003. But in fact, a dozen or more individuals profiled remain active in television broadcasting today.

Thomas A. DeLong

Introduction

Radio broadcast giants, NBC and CBS, and their research arms engaged in experimental telecasts in the 1930s. The slow technical development of transmission and reception held the television medium in abeyance for most of that decade. But, in 1938, a mobile TV van appeared on New York streets as part of its field testing, traveling the city to experiment with outdoor pickups of parades, sports events, even fires. The van had Radio Corporation of America and NBC logos which attracted much attention by the public. The following year, 1939, RCA announced the manufacture and sale of TV sets, but with reception limited to a distance of 50 or so miles from midtown Manhattan.

Television's first major step forward came with the opening of the 1939 New York World's Fair. NBC moved its cameras onto the fairgrounds to beam inaugural ceremonies to the 500 or fewer TV set owners in the metropolitan area. At the Fair's opening dedication event, Franklin Delano Roosevelt became the first U.S. president to appear on television.

At his side RCA president David Sarnoff remarked, "Now at last we add sight to sound," and so NBC began 30 hours per week of regularly scheduled — but by FCC decree — unsponsored programming. After two years of "firsts" on the small screen and breaking new ground, telecasters got the go-ahead from the FCC to move into commercial programs in 1941. Procter and Gamble, Lever Brothers and Sunoco were among the earliest sponsors.

Then shortly after the U.S. entered World War II, the federal government ruled out TV broadcasting and the manufacture of television receivers. This four-year ban ended in late 1945, and television soon embraced what would become the rudiments of its golden age. Westport and Weston, Connecticut contributed a fair number of on-camera pioneers to the fledgling medium.

Not long after the end of World War II, television began to come into its own as an important household entertainment and informational medium. Radio, of course, still remained dominant in the home, as it had for several decades. Yet a number of radio and stage performers cautiously went before the still-rudimentary TV cameras and banks of brutally hot arc lights. And the makeup required was a departure: black or dark green lipstick because red appeared white on early TV sets. For many it was a challenge, an adventure, with little remuneration beyond perhaps a bag of products from the sponsor — if the station was lucky enough to sign one up.

By 1949, TV channels in metropolitan New York numbered six, making the city the leading center for telecasts in the country, with programs virtually all "live" in that pre-taped and -edited era.

Westport and Weston had already the well-deserved reputation as home to artists and entertainers. Among them were a handful of now-nearly-forgotten video pioneers — musicologist Sigmund Spaeth, journalist Bill Leonard, photographer Victor Keppler — who established a foothold in the TV studios. These individuals, Westport and Weston neighbors, on TV blazed a trail in their commitment to a new, untried electronic receiver, which many tagged "radio with pictures."

In the 1950s, New York expanded as the major broadcast hub for a wide spectrum of programs: dramatic anthologies, soap operas, quiz shows, sporting events, variety shows, newscasts, and "spectaculars" of every sort. And to maintain these extensive weekly schedules, more and more actors, emcees, musicians, news journalists and sportscasters turned to the far-reaching and influential new medium. The neighboring towns of Westport and Weston, an hour or so from Manhattan, attracted many for their choice of a year-round home or summer place. Newsman Douglas Edwards, dancer Bambi Lynn, dramatist-host Rod Serling, sportscaster Jim McKay, comedienne Martha Raye — to name a few — settled in these communities. Others, such as singer James Melton and actress Eva Le Gallienne, already had roots in the area. With the prestigious Emmy Awards for achievements in television established in the 1950s, performers and personalities from Westport/Weston were consistently among the annual recipients.

Apart from these broadcasters, a number of writers and producers chose Westport as the setting for their sitcoms. *I Love Lucy* focused on Westport when in 1957 Lucy and Desi moved from Manhattan to "the country." *Bewitched* and *My World and Welcome to It* similarly had their whereabouts in this town, though none of these programs were actually filmed on Westport locations.

First TV Owner

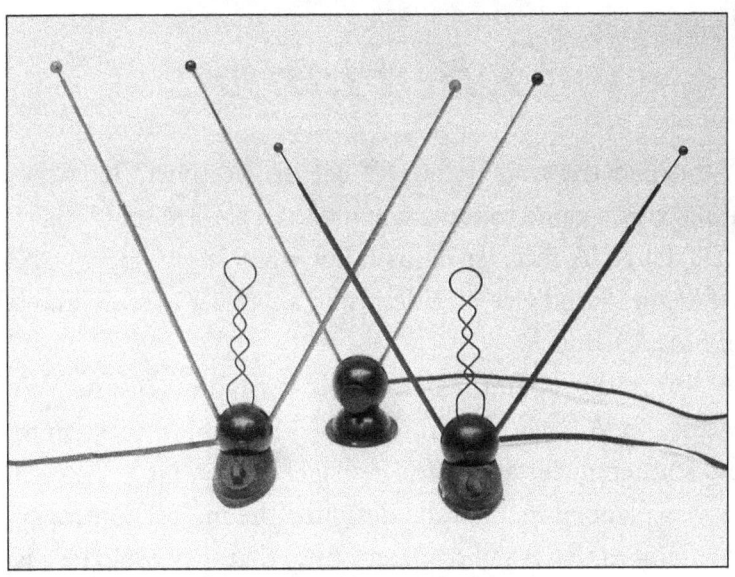

Three Antennas, Circa 1950.

O.B. Hanson

Who had the first home TV set in Westport? It is thought that television came to town when OSCAR B. HANSON (1894-1961) installed a RCA receiver in his home in 1938-39. He was NBC's chief engineer and vice president, and a pioneer in radio and television broadcasting.

A ship radio operator before joining radio stations WAAM Newark and WEAF New York in the 1920s, Hanson soon rose to NBC staff engineer and plant manager. When New York's Radio City was planned in 1931, he designed the master control system and studios for RCA radio operations so that they could be adapted for television in future years. Hanson held many patents, and is credited with the TV mobile transmitter. His skill and foresight brought workable TV broadcasting over the airwaves by the end of the 1930s.

O.B. HANSON with iconoscope camera tube that made electronic television possible. *Photo courtesy of David Sarnoff Library, Princeton, NJ.*

Pioneers

Delco TV-71 (1948).

Victor Keppler

Commercial photographer VICTOR KEPPLER (1904-1987) achieved renown as a photographic illustrator of such products as Lucky Strike cigarettes, Schaefer beer and Lux soap. In 1947 he joined photojournalist Mabel Scacheri as a participant in *Photographic Horizons*, a low-budget, live-performance instructional series for DuMont television's WABD, broadcasted from its studio in Wanamaker's department store, New York. "It was obvious that the TV camera had become a first-class teaching, as well as entertainment, tool," Keppler observed.

While in Westport in the 1960s, he co-founded, with illustrator Albert Dorne, the Famous Photographers School to teach the photographic arts through home-study courses.

Keppler also did cover photos for *The Saturday Evening Post* and wrote *The Eighth Art, a Life of Color Photography*.

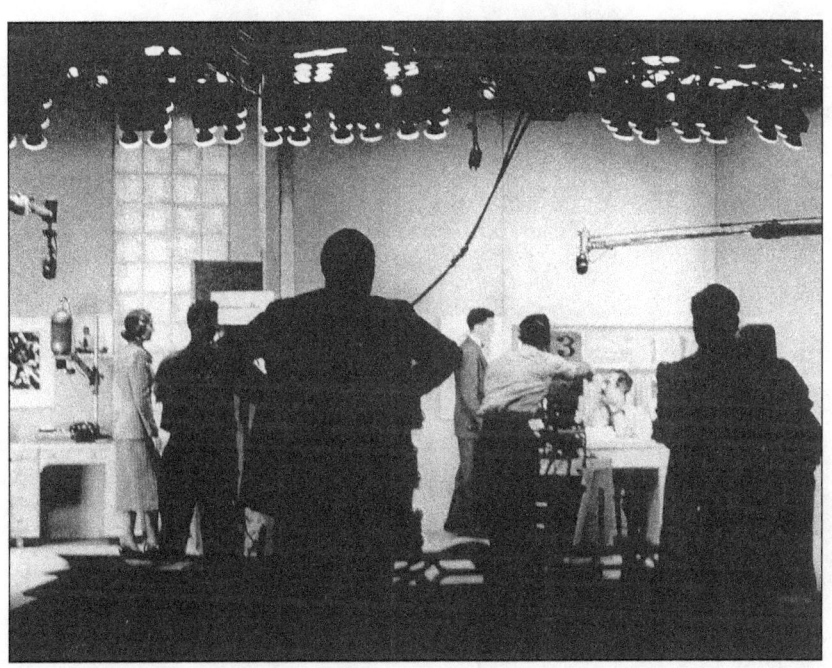

VICTOR KEPPLER on the set, *Photographic Horizons*, DuMont network (1947).

Sigmund Spaeth

Musicologist SIGMUND SPAETH (1885-1965) popularized the roots of songs in a presentation called *The Tune Detective*, in vaudeville, lectures and radio. He once traced the music lines of the madcap 1920s song "Yes, We Have No Bananas" to Handel's "Messiah" and Wagnerian operas.

A television pioneer in the 1940s with his *Tune Detective* appearances, he revealed that even the most elaborate classical works were based on simple melodies. He also urged enthusiastic amateurs to take up a musical instrument. Dr. Spaeth wrote over 30 books on practically every aspect of music. His *Music for Fun* was both a book and a broadcast series.

A Westporter since the early 1920s, he became the first musical director for the Westport Country Playhouse, and he composed a Shakespearean song for Romney Brent to sing in *As You Like It* and arranged sailors' choruses for Ibsen's *Pillars of Society*.

SIGMUND SPAETH (left) and TV musical director Johnny Green.

Dorothy Bryce

Best known for her theatre and cabaret appearances, DOROTHY BRYCE (1923-2009) was in on the ground floor of primetime and daytime television in New York. She played Rose Ryan on *The Doctors*, and had roles on the soaps *As the World Turns*, *Edge of Night* and *Young Dr. Malone*. Featured regularly on *Studio One*, *The United States Steel Hour*, *Suspense* and *You Are There*, Dorothy can still be seen on reruns of *The Sgt. Bilko Show* with Phil Silvers.

Her "live" TV commercials form an early and unique part of the medium. She became the "hands" of Arlene Francis on NBC's *Home Show*. Usually only her hands were seen by viewers. "I was always the woman too stupid to use the sponsor's product," she recalled. "I did Spic and Span commercials, and for a year had the dirtiest floor and used the wrong mop every time." The 3M Company also signed her to do commercials on *The Today Show* with Dave Garroway.

In 2006 she starred with James Noble in the film *Glacier Bay*, a tender and funny portrait of two combative seniors. She was named Best Actress at the Breckenridge Film Festival.

Born in a show-business family, Dorothy met husband Ed Bryce while searching for a leading man for her Greenwich Village Mews Playhouse in 1948. Ed not only got the part but his own leading lady! Together, they became one of Westport's most community-spirited couples, producing fundraising variety shows for their church and many non-profit organizations

DOROTHY BRYCE performing at a fundraiser cabaret celebrating the 70th anniversary of the Westport Country Playhouse. Shown with her are Wally Woods (left) and Tom DeLong (right).

Bill Leonard

BILL LEONARD (1916-1994) lived in Westport as a teenager in the 1930s and after Dartmouth came back to work as a reporter for the *Bridgeport Post-Telegram*. His journalistic career in 1945 led him to CBS where he wanted to be in television, which then barely existed. A radio series, *This is New York*, did lead to TV two years later, with his *Eye on New York* — a public service/human interest program.

In 1950 Leonard added *6 O'Clock Report*. A stalwart of TV journalism's first generation, he moved into management as vice president, later president, of CBS News, where he helped launch *60 Minutes* and its video magazine concept in 1965.

Leonard received several Emmys and the Peabody Award for Lifetime Achievement in Broadcasting.

BILL LEONARD hosts *Eye on New York*, an early public service program.

Win Elliot

Radio treated WIN ELLIOT (1915-1998) very well. He presided over many audience participation shows and interviewed guests on daily homemaker programs for a decade or more. Win hustled for jobs in every direction, and when TV came on the scene, he jumped in. A new channel, WPIX New York, in 1948 gave him his first sports assignment, a Rangers hockey game. He did play-by-play for all of the first baseball games on TV from Yankee Stadium.

"The top sportscasters wouldn't touch TV in those days because the money was nothing," Win recalled. "But I wanted to do sports." He soon handled telecasts of boxing, track & field, bowling and horse racing, his favorite sport along with hockey. He also hosted *Schaefer Circle of Sports*.

During TV's early quiz craze, Elliot emceed *Tic Tac Dough*, *On Your Account* and *Win With a Winner*, a program he created in 1958.

A longtime, much-admired Westport-Weston resident, he began his broadcast career at a small Boston station with his good high baritone voice and a solid fund of general knowledge, ambition and perseverance.

WIN ELLIOT and Elinor Ames lead an etiquette discussion on *The Correct Thing* at WPIX (1952).

Eva Le Gallienne

Videotaped performances preserve a number of the extraordinary stage roles of legendary Broadway star EVA LE GALLIENNE (1899-1991). She generally resisted appearing before TV cameras in a studio without an audience. However as early as the 1947-48 season, she was persuaded to co-star in the CBS production of *Years Ago* with Raymond Massey.

Beginning in the 1950s, she reprised versions of her classic theatre plays: "Uncle Harry" (*Ford Television Theatre*), "Alice in Wonderland" (*Hallmark Hall of Fame*), "The Bridge of San Luis Rey" (*DuPont Show of the Month*) and "Mary Stuart" (*Play of the Week*). She performed a scene from "Camille" on *Ed Sullivan's Toast of the Town* for the then-top fee of $1,000.

In 1977 PBS filmed the successful revival of "The Royal Family" for its *Great Performances* series. For her work Eva Le Gallienne won an Emmy as best supporting actress in a comedy special. Her final performance proved to be in an episode of *St. Elsewhere* at age 85.

EVA LE GALLIENNE (right), Emmy award for "The Royal Family," PBS's *Great Performances,* with Rosemary Harris, Ellis Rabb (1977).

John Lodge

TV broadcasting came to England in 1936, several years before arriving in the United States. While making movies in and about London, JOHN LODGE (1903-1985) appeared on several BBC telecasts. Perhaps the first American actor to do TV overseas, he was seen on *Round the Film Studios* in 1937, direct from Pinewood and Elstree studios. Later, he made a similar guest appearance on *Picture Parade*.

The longtime Westport actor-turned-politico also became a pioneer in U.S. television of the early 1950s. As Governor he inaugurated a weekly series of TV programs on Connecticut governmental departments and agencies. With various officials, he reviewed the scope of services offered by Motor Vehicle, Mental Health, Public Works and other units. One of the first in any state to utilize TV on a regular and informative public-service basis, Governor Lodge during his term (1951-55) also created a Commission of Education Television.

JOHN LODGE (right) in 1937 when making British TV appearances, with Ed Black, Francesca Lodge, Carol Reed.

Drama

RCA Victor 630TS (1946).

Bette Davis

With two Oscars on her mantle, BETTE DAVIS (1908-1989) also made her mark on television, receiving an Emmy for the lead in the 1979 special *Strangers: The Story of a Mother and Daughter*. She was signed for a recurring role as hotel owner Laura Trent in the drama series *Hotel*, but due to illness was only seen on the premiere in 1983. Her character then departed on an "extended trip," leaving her sister-in-law, Victoria Cabot (Anne Baxter), in charge.

As a major Hollywood star, Davis took on guest appearances in dramatic anthologies such as *General Electric Theatre*, *DuPont Show with June Allyson*, and on the international intrigue series *It Takes a Thief* with Robert Wagner. For comedy relief she joined the revived *Laugh-In* show, sharing the screen with no fewer than five Bette Davis imitators.

Bette Davis is a part of Westport-Weston history, having been active in community fundraisers and art festivals during her years as a resident of both towns from 1968 into the 1980s.

BETTE DAVIS in her Emmy-winning role in *Strangers, The Story of a Mother and Daughter* with Gena Rowlands (1979).

Joanne Woodward

A young stage actress working in New York, JOANNE WOODWARD broke into TV with the lead in "Welcome Home" on *The Web* in 1954. Important roles followed in numerous drama series: *Ponds Theatre, Star Tonight, Kraft Theatre* and *Alcoa Hour*.

Films in Hollywood launched Woodward's international career, and won her an Oscar for *Three Faces of Eve* in 1957. She co-starred in a half-dozen pictures with husband Paul Newman (*From the Terrace, Mr. & Mrs. Bridge*). He also directed her in the Oscar-nominated *Rachel, Rachel*.

Woodward received two Emmys for lead actress in drama specials: "See How She Runs" (1978) on *GE Theatre* and *Do You Remember Love?* (1985). She hosted and produced *Dance in America: Bob Fosse Steam Heat*, which won an Emmy as outstanding informational special in 1990.

Joanne has often directed plays, most recently at the Westport Country Playhouse, where she was artistic director. A Westport resident for some 50 years, she has devoted considerable energy to various dance companies and local arts and medical research projects.

JOANNE WOODWARD in an Emmy-winning role for CBS dramatic special *Do You Remember Love?* with Richard Kiley (1985).

John Malkovich

With stellar turns on stage (*True West*) and screen (*Places in the Heart*) JOHN MALKOVICH has added director to his list of achievements. The quirky, taciturn performer and, in his words "no matinee idol," has ventured into television infrequently. But when he does, it is usually a didactic portrayal.

In 1981 Malkovich appeared in the TV films *Word of Honor* and *American Dreams*. Four years later he played Biff in *Death of a Salesman*, a three-hour dramatic special on CBS. The role brought him an Emmy for outstanding supporting actor. He followed up in the 1990s with *Heart of Darkness* and *Napoleon* (as Talleyrand).

The film *Being John Malkovich* elevated his public persona, but by choice he has long avoided celebrity status.

Other notable big screen roles include *Empire of the Sun*, directed by Steven Spielberg; *In the Line of Fire*, an Oscar-nominated role; and *Dangerous Liaisons*, co-starring Michelle Pfeiffer. John lived and worked in France for nearly a decade, but earlier in his career he spent time at his summer home in Weston.

JOHN MALKOVICH as Biff, Stephen Lang as Happy, in the Emmy-winning CBS special *Death of a Salesman* (1985).

Shirley Knight

A Tony recipient and Oscar nominee, SHIRLEY KNIGHT has made an impression with TV viewers in Emmy-winning roles. This renowned actress won her first Emmy as outstanding guest performer in the drama series *thirtysomething* in 1988. Her second award for supporting actress came for the special program *Indictment: The McMartin Trial* for HBO in 1995.

Producers have cast Shirley in such dramatic specials as *The Defection of Simas Kudirka* and TV films, including *Champion*. She played roles on *The Virginian, ER, Desperate Housewives, Playhouse 90, Naked* City and *The Fugitive*. And for the BBC she starred in tele-features written by her late husband, playwright John Hopkins.

Kansas-born Knight has fared less successfully in ongoing series. At CBS *Angel Falls* (1993) and *Maggie Winters* (1998-99) with Faith Ford were short-lived.

Westport has been her home base between career assignments in Hollywood and London.

SHIRLEY KNIGHT, Alan Arkin, *The Defection of Simas Kudirka*, CBS dramatic special (1980).

Dana Andrews

The film career of DANA ANDREWS (1909-1992) drew critical acclaim and public favor, highlighted by leads as the sturdy archetypical hero of *A Walk in the Sun, Laura* and *The Best Years of Our Lives*. But by the end of the 1950s, he had trouble obtaining the movie roles he wanted. Producers were also cutting back on the medium-budget films in which he had established himself.

Television was not something Andrews especially liked. He appeared in the short series *Ike*. From 1969 to 1972, as his career faded, he starred in the NBC daytime serial *Bright Promise*, portraying a college president involved in the struggle of change in small-town academia.

Andrews called TV "just an adjunct of the advertising business," and welcomed a chance to return to movies with *Airport 1975* and *The Last Tycoon*. During his TV and Broadway stints he lived in Weston, but spent his last years in California.

DANA ANDREWS and Coleen Gray, daytime series *Bright Promise*.

Alan Arkin

ALAN ARKIN, star of the critically acclaimed series *100 Centre Street*, worked in a Queens, NY, TV studio and lived in an oriental-style house in Weston. The role of Judge Joe Rifkind with his big-city, gritty dialogue was tailor-made for the New York-born actor/director/writer. Two of his sons, Adam and Matt, have appeared on *Centre Street*.

Earlier, Arkin portrayed a wheeler-dealer hospital supply clerk in the short-lived ABC comedy, *Harry*. In 1966 he received an Emmy nomination for his performance in a drama on *ABC Stage* and in 1987 for the special *Escape from Sobibor*.

An original member of Chicago's Second City troupe, he made his debut on Broadway in *Enter Laughing* and in films with *The Russians are Coming, The Russians are Coming*, for which he received an Oscar nomination. In 2007 he won an Academy Award as Best Supporting Actor for *Little Miss Sunshine*.

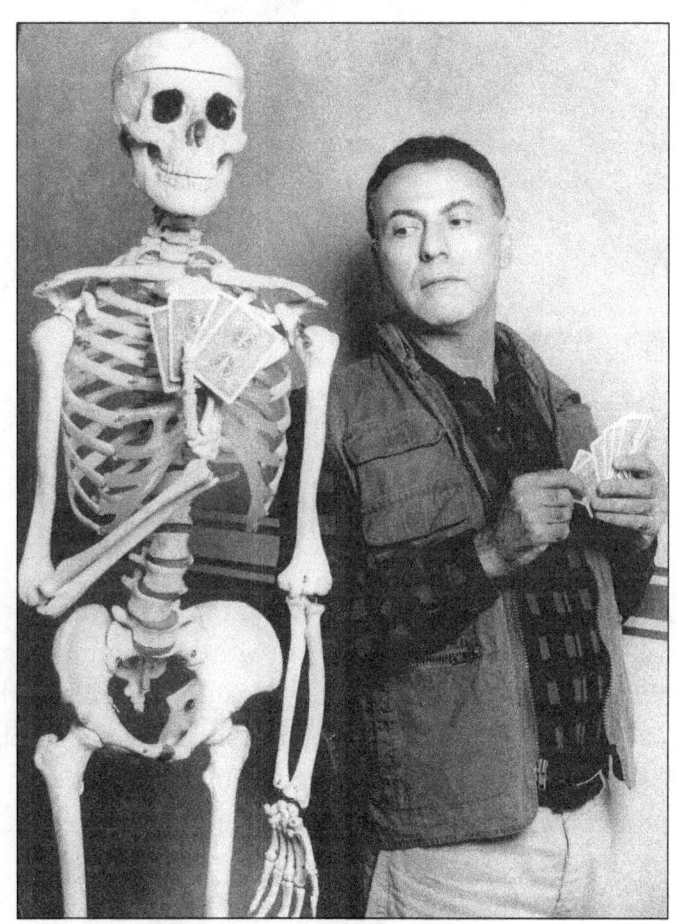

ALAN ARKIN, lead in the sitcom *Harry* (1987).

Mia Farrow

At age 18 while beginning her acting career in New York and living on Easton Road in Westport (with her mother Maureen O'Sullivan), MIA FARROW was asked to test for the pilot of the TV series *Peyton Place*, based on the notoriously successful novel. Playing Allison, she helped attract a large following for what in effect was a primetime soap opera that ran three times a week on ABC in the 1960s.

By the time Mia cut her waist-length hair and left the show for films, she had become an international celebrity from dubbed overseas runs of *Peyton Place*.

The doe-like actress made her mark in pictures as the victim of devil worshippers in *Rosemary's Baby*. She played leads in 13 movies — including *Hannah and Her Sisters*, *Alice* and *Broadway Danny Rose*, all directed by Woody Allen (her lover until their infamous break-up in 1996).

A UNICEF Special Representative, Mia was a UN Goodwill Ambassador to Central African Republic and Chad in 2007. She was selected by *Time Magazine* as one of the most influential people in the world in 2008.

MIA FARROW and Ryan O'Neal were a romantic duo on *Peyton Place* (1964-1966).

Tina Louise

In the mid-1950s actress-singer TINA LOUISE divided her time between TV dramas and supper club bookings. Roles on *Studio One* and *Appointment with Adventure* and vocal appearances on *Jan Murray Time* led to Broadway (*Li'l Abner*) and films (*God's Little Acre*).

The statuesque Westport debutante achieved her greatest, and seemingly lasting, fame as Ginger, the voluptuous movie star stranded for three seasons (1964-67) on *Gilligan's Island*. Originally beamed to youngsters, it became a cult classic for all ages and remains one of TV's biggest rerun hits.

In subsequent decades, Tina was seen on *Dallas* during its first season (1978-79) and on *Rituals*, a syndicated drama featuring Dennis Patrick.

TINA LOUISE shipwrecked on *Gilligan's Island*, with Alan Hale, Jr. and Bob Denver (1964-1967).

Carole Shelley

CAROLE SHELLEY made her New York stage debut as Gwendolyn Pigeon in Neil Simon's *The Odd Couple,* reprised the role of the dizzy English girl in the film, and in 1970 was featured in the TV series. Gwendolyn and her sister Cecily were the Pigeon Sisters who came to New York to work and live, sharing an apartment upstairs in Felix and Oscar's building.

English-born Shelley remains active on Broadway where she won a Tony for *The Elephant Man*, and on the London stage with *Lettice and Lovage* and *Show Boat*.

She has co-starred in network television pilots and daytime dramas, including *One Life to Live* and *All My Children*. She has been seen on *Spencer: For Hire* and *The Cosby Show*. A mainstay of Shakespeare Festivals in New York and Ontario, Shelley created the role of Madame Morrible in the 2003 musical *Wicked*, and later played Grandma in the New York production of *Billy Elliot*.

She has been a Westporter since the 1980s.

CAROLE SHELLEY (left) and Monica Evans played the Pigeon Sisters on *The Odd Couple* (1970-1971).

David Wayne

In the 1947-48 season, actor DAVID WAYNE (1914-1995) co-starred with Gertrude Lawrence in *The Great Catherine,* the first play of George Bernard Shaw to be performed — with his permission — on TV. Part of a seven-play "live" series produced by The Theatre Guild, it inaugurated NBC's first full-scale video studio in New York. Wayne became a regular on the new medium, appearing on *NBC Repertory Theatre* in 1949, and played the lead in the 1955 comedy *Norby,* the first TV series to be filmed in color. Appropriately, it was sponsored by Kodak.

Between award-winning performances on Broadway (*Finian's Rainbow, The Happy Time*) and top roles in 20th Century-Fox films (*The Three Faces of Eve, How to Marry a Millionaire*), the versatile Wayne came into millions of homes as Inspector Richard Queen for *The Adventures of Ellery Queen,* Digger Barnes in *Dallas,* the Mad Hatter in *Batman,* Dr. Weatherby for *House Calls,* and industrialist Charlie Dutton of *The Good Life.*

Wayne moved his family from Manhattan to Westport's Old Hill area in 1953 and stayed there until the late 1970s when virtually all TV series were being broadcast from the West Coast.

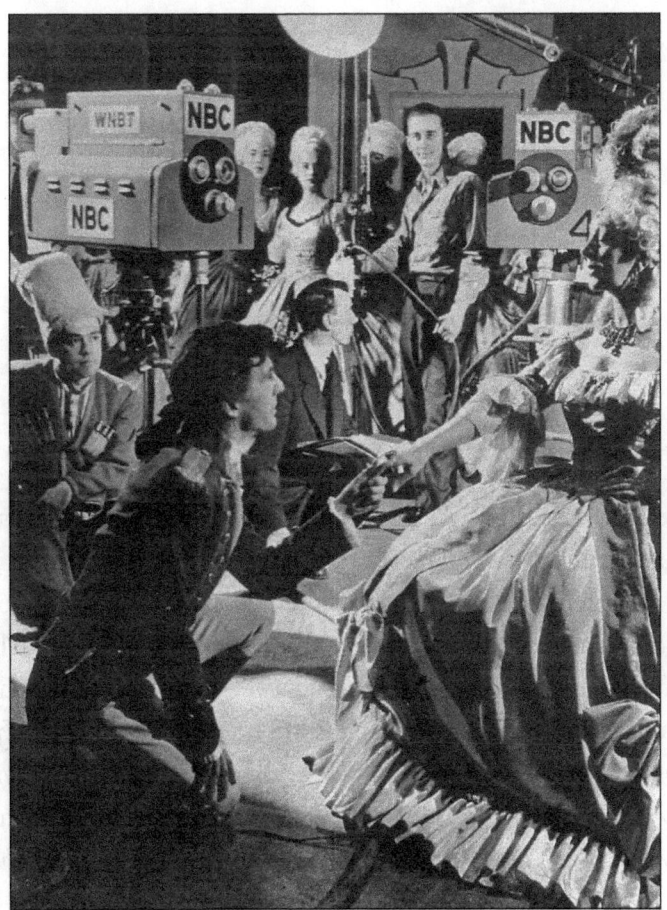

DAVID WAYNE, Gertrude Lawrence, in *The Great Catherine*, first Shaw play performed on TV (1947).

Christopher Plummer

One of the theatre's most distinguished actors, CHRISTOPHER PLUMMER has received several Tonys, a Drama Desk Award, the Edwin Booth Award for Lifetime Achievement and many other honors. His notable Shakespearean roles range from Marc Antony and Macbeth to Henry V, Iago and Lear. He is also a veteran of over 60 films since 1957, and author of the rollicking 2008 memoir *In Spite of Myself*.

The actor's TV credits include the BBC's three-hour *Hamlet at Ellsinore*, *Don Juan in Hell* and *The Thorn Birds*. He won his first Emmy in 1977 for outstanding lead actor in the series, *The Moneychangers* on NBC's *The Big Event*. He picked up a second Emmy for voiceover performance (narrator) of *Madeline* on The Family Channel in 1994. Plummer starred in 66 episodes of *Counterstrike* on the USA Network in the early 1990s, playing Toronto billionaire Alexander Addington who formed an international crime-fighting team to crack cases the authorities would not tackle.

A Canadian by birth, Plummer has lived in Weston for more than 25 years. His daughter is the noted actress Amanda Plummer.

CHRISTOPHER PLUMMER in Emmy-winning role, *The Moneychangers*, on *The Big Event* with Joan Collins, Lorne Greene (1977).

Diana Douglas

DIANA DOUGLAS started out as a New York model in the early 1940s; one of her first assignments was a pose in front of the landmark Minuteman Statue in Westport. Stage and film roles followed, as did marriage to Kirk Douglas and the birth of sons Michael and Joel Douglas.

In the 1950s she began working regularly on TV, with leads on *Studio One*, *Philco Playhouse* and *Kraft Television Theatre*. Then came the soap *Three Steps to Heaven*. Leaving New York in 1956, the now-divorced actress chose a simple white clapboard farmhouse with a red barn on Westport's Whitney Street, her country home for 20 years with new husband Bill Darrid.

Her TV credits continued with *The Defenders* and *The Cowboys*, and in the 1985-86 season with the plum role as law professor Tyler on *The Paper Chase* with John Houseman. More recently, she appeared in the film *It Runs in the Family* with Kirk Douglas, their son Michael and grandson Cameron.

DIANA DOUGLAS, John Houseman, *The Paper Chase* (1986).

Bruce Weitz

A regular on the police drama *Hill Street Blues* during its six-year run, beginning in 1981, BRUCE WEITZ played Detective Mick Betker. The part brought him a 1984 Emmy for Best Supporting Actor.

Bruce spent much of his youth in Westport, where he served as a Country Playhouse apprentice. Following stage roles, he moved to Los Angeles to get into TV episodic work. His first break was the costarring TV role in *Death of a Centerfold: The Dorothy Stratton Story*, as Stratton's husband. Then came *Hill Street Blues*, considered one of the most influential programs ever on TV.

In the 1990s he appeared in the sitcom *Anything But Love* and family drama *Byrds of Paradise*, filmed in Hawaii. In 2007 he began a role on *General Hospital*.

BRUCE WEITZ gained national recognition as Mick on *Hill Street Blues* (1981-1987).

Michael Douglas

From the streets of Westport in the 1950s — chiefly Whitney Street — to TV's *Streets of San Francisco* in the 1970s, MICHAEL DOUGLAS launched a formidable film career by first acting on television. His break came when he was cast in the *CBS Playhouse* production of the drama *The Experiment* in 1969, garnering glowing reviews as a free-spirited scientist.

A handful of movies and TV assignments led to the part of Karl Malden's sidekick, Inspector Steve Keller, in *Streets of San Francisco* at ABC. This duo on the top-rated police series earned Emmy nominations in three successive seasons (1972-74).

Film work attracted Douglas, who produced the screen version of *One Flew Over the Cuckoo's Nest*. It won five Academy Awards, and placed him in the upper echelon of actor-producer.

The son of actors Kirk Douglas and Diana Douglas Darrid, Michael, along with his brother Joel, spent his formative years in Connecticut.

MICHAEL DOUGLAS, Karl Malden,
The Streets of San Francisco (1972-1976).

Frank Lovejoy

A lead in numerous dramatic presentations, beginning on radio in New York in the late 1930s, FRANK LOVEJOY (1912- 1962) com muted there from a house on Bayberry Lane. He and his wife, the actress Joan Banks, lived in Westport until he entered films with *Home of the Brave* in 1949.

Soon TV audiences saw the rugged tough guy in the detective series *Man Against Crime* (1956). Lovejoy had a longer run as McGraw, a private eye who accepted all sorts of dangerous pursuits on *Meet McGraw*, from 1957 to 1959.

His most enduring stage portrayal was as an unscrupulous political candidate in Gore Vidal's *The Best Man*.

FRANK LOVEJOY on *Meet McGraw*, detective drama (1957-1959).

Mason Adams

A bicoastal journeyman actor, MASON ADAMS (1919-2005) had numerous credits in theatre, film, radio and television, believing it was the part and the writing that mattered in his long and successful career. Best known to millions of Americans as managing editor Charlie Hume on TV's *Lou Grant* (1977-1982), he earned three Emmy nominations for that role. He later costarred on the sitcom *Knight & Daye* with Jack Warden. Adams has done TV movies and numerous commercials, most notably as the spokesman for Smucker's jams and jellies.

A leading radio soap star as Pepper Young (*Pepper Young's Family*) in his early years, he appeared in William Saroyan and Arthur Miller plays on Broadway and in *Foxfire* here on the summer circuit. Adams made Westport his home base for decades.

MASON ADAMS, Ed Asner, Nancy Marchand on *Lou Grant* (1977-1982).

Mariette Hartley

Her first TV exposure was as Dr. Claire Morton on *Peyton Place* in 1965. Weston-raised, Staples High School-educated, MARIETTE HARTLEY had started her career with the iconic film *Ride the High Country* at age 19. But TV made her known to millions of fans. *The Hero*, a sitcom in 1966-67, costarred her with Richard Mulligan. *Goodnight, Beantown* in the 1980s cast her opposite Bill Bixby in a Boston TV newsroom setting with parallels to Mary Tyler Moore's newsroom series. She briefly co-hosted the *CBS Early Show*.

Hartley became a household name in the '80s from the award-winning Polaroid commercials she did with James Garner. They also worked together on his TV programs. She received a 1979 Emmy as outstanding lead actress in *The Incredible Hulk* series episode, "Married."

In the 1990s Mariette was seen on *WIOU* and *Caroline in the City* (as Lea Thompson's mother) and as host of *Healthy Solutions* for CNBC. She played on Broadway in *Cabaret*, and came back to Weston to talk on alcohol and drug awareness programs from personal experience, stressing the need for intervention and open communication.

MARIETTE HARTLEY in her Emmy-winning performance in "Married," *The Incredible Hulk* with Bill Bixby.

Darren McGavin

To many viewers in the 1950s, DARREN MCGAVIN (1922-2006) did his best work as the tough-talking private eye in *Mickey Spillane's Mike Hammer*. Roles as TV detective were repeated on *The Outsider* and *Small & Frye*. And McGavin played a crime reporter on *Kolchak: The Night Stalker* (1974-75) and newspaper photographer Casey on *Crime Photographer* (1951-52), his earliest TV lead. He sailed onto home screens as Captain Grey Holden of the "Enterprise" on *Riverboat*.

The stage and films remained an important segment of his acting credits. On Broadway he did *My Three Angels* and *The Rainmaker*, and in Hollywood, *Summertime*, *The Man with the Golden Arm* and portrayed the grouchy dad in the holiday classic *A Christmas Story*.

Darren handled both dramatic and comedy parts on TV's *Chrysler Theatre* and *CBS Summer Playhouse*, and hosted the supernatural anthology *Miracles and Other Wonders*. In 1990 he won the Emmy as the opinionated father of *Murphy Brown*.

The McGavin family lived on Old Mill Road in what is woefully remembered as the tallest house in that Westport area, the outcome in a zoning dispute over whether he could add an extra floor onto his house.

DARREN McGAVIN as *Casey, Crime Photographer* (1951-1952).

Pamela Sue Martin

Although her well-remembered *Nancy Drew Mysteries* lasted only for a year or so, beginning in 1977, PAMELA SUE MARTIN is indelibly linked to that starring role of the fearless teenage sleuth who motored about in a blue roadster solving crimes. The series grew from the string of enduring Nancy Drew books that young girls have scooped up by the millions since 1930.

The Sunday evening program alternated with ABC's *Hardy Boys Mysteries*, a similar adventure program. Pamela Sue appeared in several joint episodes with the teenage Hardy sons, played by Shaun Cassidy and Parker Stevenson.

She grew up in Westport and graduated from Staples High. Her earliest work was as a teenage model in magazine ads and TV commercials. Favorable notices from the films *To Find a Man* and *The Poseidon Adventure* led to TV cameras and movies for television. The PBS production, *The Hemingway Play*, is among her favorites.

In the early 1980s she joined the cast of the primetime soap *Dynasty* for the role of Fallon Carrington Colby, the spoiled, arrogant daughter of oil magnate Blake (John Forsythe). From there the athletic Pamela Sue co-hosted *The Star Games* with Bruce Jenner in 26 syndicated episodes of sports events featuring actors from different TV series.

PAMELA SUE MARTIN brought the teenage Nancy Drew detective to the TV screen (1977-1978).

Jack Klugman

Hollywood Screen Test, the first regular series on the ABC network, showcased new talent looking for the "big break." Hosted by Neil Hamilton, it discovered JACK KLUGMAN in the early 1950s (along with Jack Lemmon, Grace Kelly and Betsy Palmer). Skilled in drama and comedy, this actor with the glum growl became enormously productive in television. His supporting roles took off with *Treasury Men in Action*, based on actual cases and telecast live. His appearances on the 1964 episode entitled "Blacklist" on *The Defenders*, with E. G. Marshall, won Klugman an Emmy. The same year he starred in the sitcom *Harris Against the World*.

The Odd Couple comedy first aired in 1970 with Klugman as the gruff, sloppy Oscar (and Tony Randall as prim, fastidious Felix). The series delighted viewers for five seasons and brought Jack two more best actor Emmys. He next moved onto the popular police drama *Quincy, M.E.* playing a medical examiner in the LA Coroner's office. In the 1980s he starred as supermarket manager Henry Willows on *You Again?* and later in *The Odd Couple Returns* at CBS.

This erstwhile Weston neighbor has solid credits on stage (*Gypsy*) and in film (*Days of Wine and Roses*).

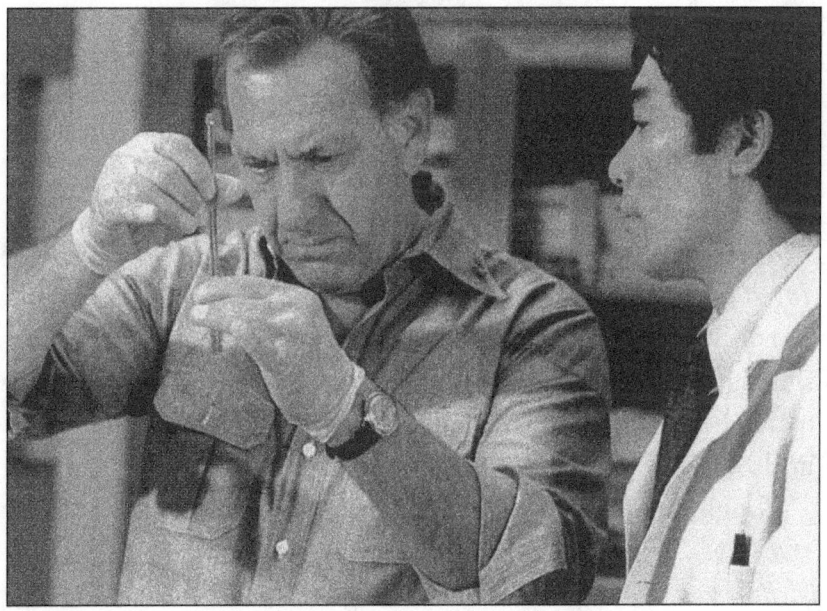

JACK KLUGMAN as *Quincy, M.E.* (1976-1983).

James Naughton

An actor-singer with two Tonys for Broadway musicals (*City of Angels* and *Chicago*) JAMES NAUGHTON has been on stage, in film and on TV for over three decades. He's often taping in the morning, singing in the evening, and directing in-between. A Connecticut native, he began acting while in high school at West Hartford, then in Brown and Yale School of Drama productions.

Naughton has been doing television series since the 1970s: *Planet of the Apes*, *Who's the Boss?*, *Brooklyn Bridge*, and more recently *Ally McBeal* and *Damages*. Films, too, range from *The Glass Menagerie* with Joanne Woodward and directed by Paul Newman, *The Paper Chase*, *First Wives Club* and *The Devil Wears Prada* opposite Meryl Streep.

A Weston resident, he has performed in *Ancestral Voices* and in his one-man cabaret *Street of Dreams* at the Westport Country Playhouse. His directing there of the 2002 revival of *Our Town*, starring Paul Newman, helped move it to Broadway for a sold-out limited run. This production was also filmed for public television.

JAMES NAUGHTON, Ron Harper, on an Earth of the future in *Planet of the Apes* (1974).

David Marshall Grant

A considerable segment of actor-playwright DAVID MARSHALL GRANT's career has focused on TV movies, beginning with *Kent State* and *Legs* in the early 1980s. His magnetic TV roles continued as Robert Kennedy in *Citizen Cohn* and as a sly Nazi in *Breaking Point*. A versatile actor, he played a gay man who enters the yuppie sphere of pals on the acclaimed *thirtysomething* in 1989. During the 1997-98 season he appeared as an untypical Catholic cleric on ABC's religious drama *Nothing Sacred*, starring Kevin Anderson.

Grant broke into the professional ranks in 1978, the year he graduated from Yale School of Drama with *Bent* on Broadway opposite Richard Gere. He was nominated for a Tony for his performance in *Angels in America*. His films include *French Postcards, American Flyers* and *The Rock*.

During his summer break from Staples High School in the early '70s, he studied at Juilliard. He wrote a play, *Snakebite*, which received 1999 Drama Desk and Outer Critics Circle award nominations. He continues as a performer, a screenwriter, a story editor and a series producer.

Michael Hayden

Staples Players alumnus and Juilliard graduate MICHAEL HAYDEN achieved star status as Billy Bigelow in the London and New York productions of *Carousel*. A decade of leads followed on Broadway with *Cabaret, Enchanted April* and *Judgment at Nuremberg*, for which he received a Tony nomination. Regional credits range from Tennessee Williams' *Sweet Bird of Youth* to Sondheim's *Merrily We Roll Along*.

In 1995 Hayden made his first TV appearance as Richard Crenna's crippled grandson in the telefilm *In the Name of Love: A Texas Tragedy*.

His 1995-1997 TV role as lawyer Chris Docknovitch in the ABC legal drama *Murder One* was critically acclaimed. Hayden has been seen on *Bella Mafia, Hack, Law & Order*, and the PBS presentation of *Far East*, as well as in many soaps.

He starred opposite his wife, British actress Elizabeth Sastre, in *Camila* (2001), a musical mix of love and religion in 1840s Argentina. They now live in London.

Joan Banks

Character actress JOAN BANKS (1918-1998) frequently appeared in TV episodes of *Perry Mason*, and as Sylvia opposite Ann Sothern in the 1950s comedy series *Private Secretary*. She also was in the cast of the serial *Love of Life*, beginning in 1970.

Banks started her career on radio where she worked on *Gangbusters* and *This Day is Ours*, both with Frank Lovejoy. They married in 1940, and shortly thereafter settled in Westport on Bayberry Lane. Her broadcast credits included the role of Jane, roommate of *My Friend Irma* (played by comedienne Marie Wilson).

Frank Converse

FRANK CONVERSE's TV appearances range from series and pilots to movies and miniseries. His initial run on *Coronet Blue* in 1967 was quickly followed by two seasons (1967-69) as Detective Johnny Corso on *N.Y.P.D.* Between film and stage appearances, he returned to the home screen for the NBC adventure *Movin' On* and drama *The Family Tree*.

Frank has been a staple of the soap world with *One Life to Live* and *All My Children*. His TV movies include *Dr. Cook's Garden, Cruise into Terror, Home at Last* and as Joe DiMaggio in *Marilyn: The Untold Story* in 1980. Episodic appearances on *Hotel, Law & Order, The Practice* and other major drama series are frequent for this St. Louis-born actor.

Converse, nonetheless, prefers the challenge of the stage with live audiences, and has done Broadway and regional theatre. Living in Weston with his wife, the actress Maureen Anderman, he's had a number of major roles at the Westport Country Playhouse, including the highly acclaimed *Our Town* in 2002.

FRANK CONVERSE with sidekick Claude Akins, *Movin' On* (1974-1976).

June Havoc

Starting her career as a dancer in vaudeville and an actress in a stock company, JUNE HAVOC (1912-2010) made her mark on Broadway (*Pal Joey, Mexican Hayride*), and in films (*My Sister Eileen* and her best received performance in *Gentleman's Agreement*).

She was depicted in the fictionalized portrayal of her as Baby June in the 1959 musical hit *Gypsy*, a production that chiefly focused on her sister, striptease artist Gypsy Rose Lee, and their mother, Mama Rose.

In the post-war decade of early television viewers saw her in the lead in *Willy*, a sitcom about Willa Dodger, a lawyer, and her boyfriend Charlie, played by Whit Connor. Guest roles on the dramatic anthologies *Panic* and *General Electric Theatre* (hosted by Ronald Reagan) displayed her star quality. Her final TV work at age 77 was in daytime's *General Hospital*.

A Tony-nominated director of her autobiographical play, *Marathon '33*, Havoc wrote two well-received books on her life in show business. Born in Canada, she lived in many parts of the United States but for over 40 years made Westport and surrounding communities her home.

JUNE HAVOC stars in *Willy* with Whit Connor (1955).

Paul Newman

PAUL NEWMAN (1925-2008) made his film debut (*The Silver Chalice*) in 1955, but a half-dozen years earlier he began working in television as Nels's friend in *I Remember Mama*. A string of roles in "live" TV dramas in the 1950s ranged from "The Fate of Nathan Hale" for *You Are There* to "The Eighty Yard Run" on *Playhouse 90*, and "Bridge of the Devil" for *Appointment with Adventure*.

Yet it was the part of George Gibbs, the doctor's son, in *Producers' Showcase* "Our Town" (1955) that remains a high point in early TV, giving Newman an opportunity to sing in this 90-minute musical adaptation with Frank Sinatra and Eva Marie Saint. 47 years later, Oscar-winner Paul Newman returned to *Our Town* in the key role of Stage Manager at the Westport Country Playhouse. A hit of the 2002 summer season, he reprised the part as narrator of the story when it moved to Broadway for a limited run — and gained him a Tony nomination. When taped, then aired on PBS, it earned Newman a 2003 Emmy.

Paul and his wife of 50 years, Joanne Woodward, have been generous leaders in Westport's cultural and humanitarian programs for dozens of years. Since 1982 the Newman's Own Foundation has donated its food product profits totaling more than $300 million to multiple charities.

Paul and Joanne reared their three daughters in an antique farmhouse on 15 acres in Westport.

PAUL NEWMAN, Eva Marie Saint as George and Emily on NBC *Producers Showcase's* "Our Town" (1955).

Patricia Kalember

Born in Schenectady and raised in Westport, PATRICIA KALEMBER is best known for her role as the part-time real estate agent Georgie on the NBC serial *Sisters* (1991-96), and as Susannah Hart earlier on ABC's *thirtysomething*. She played the lead in the short-lived *Kay O'Brien*, a 1986 medical drama, and a political columnist opposite Tim Matheson in the 1988 sitcom *Just In Time*.

Kalember lately appeared in the HBO film *Path to War*, directed by John Frankenheimer, and in *Law & Order SUV* and *Early Edition*. Appearances on Broadway (*The Nerd*), off-Broadway (*The Foreigner*), and in feature films (*A Time for Dancing*) have enhanced her acting credits.

PATRICIA KALEMBER (top) with *Sisters'* Swoosie Kurtz, Julianne Phillips, Sela Ward (1991-1996)

Michael Jai White

Raised in Bridgeport and Westport, Connecticut, MICHAEL JAI WHITE started out as a junior high teacher for troubled youth. He eventually decided he had a knack for acting, after winning roles in commercials. White also had success on Broadway and on TV soaps. He was the first African American to portray a major comic book superhero on the big screen starring as Al Simmons, the protagonist in the 1997 film *Spawn*.

A professional martial artist, White has made guest appearances on *NYPD Blue*, *Living Single*, *Tyler Perry's House of Payne* and *The Legend of Bruce Lee*. He is best known for his role as heavyweight boxer Mike Tyson in the 1995 TV special *Tyson*.

White's filmography lists more than a dozen pictures, including *Breakfast of Champions*, *Exit Wounds* and *The Dark Knight*.

MICHAEL JAI WHITE in his best-known role as prizefighter Mike Tyson in *Tyson* with George C. Scott (1995).

David Rogers

During his initial acting career, DAVID ROGERS appeared in early New York-based "live" TV programs: the weekly *Lux Video Theatre* and *Philco TV Playhouse*, and the documentary drama *You Are There*, hosted by Walter Cronkite. Then came a period of writing for TV comedy series: *Carol Burnett Show*, *Timex Comedy Hour* and Jackie Gleason's *Honeymooners*. Rogers also penned the libretto for the opera *The Hero*, commissioned by Lincoln Center and then aired on PBS. It won the prestigious Prix d'Italia.

Since his return to acting, this Westporter has periodically been on Broadway and national tours. David's recent TV work includes *Law & Order* dramas and its spin-offs, *Special Victims Unit* and *Criminal Intent*.

DAVID ROGERS in *Law & Order: Criminal Intent*.

Amanda Rogers

Actress AMANDA ROGERS has regularly performed in the delightful, two-act *Groucho–A Life in Revue* with husband Frank Ferrante as the intractable Marx Brother. For PBS she wrote, directed and produced *Behind the Scenes with Groucho*, and has created other film and TV screenplays. Her television acting credits include *ER*, *Ties That Bind* and *Days of Our Lives*, and the CBS miniseries *American Tragedy: The O.J. Simpson Story*. Amanda has lent her voice to the animated series *Prince Valiant* and *The Phantom*.

She has done theatre tours (*Plaza Suite*) and stage work in comedy (*Laughter on the 23rd Floor*) and drama (*Desire under the Elm*). With her parents June and David Rogers she co-starred at the Westport Country Playhouse in *The Perfect Wedding*.

AMANDA ROGERS is welcomed as guest star by *ER*'s star George Clooney.

Dulcy Rogers

DULCY ROGERS works in TV in several different capacities. As an actress she has guest starred on *Wings*, *Pursuit of Happiness* and *Frasier*. She did several episodes of E!'s *Talk Soup*, and joined the cast for the 2001-2002 season of *The Drew Carey Show* as the girlfriend of Oswald, played by her husband Diedrich Bader, a co-star on this sitcom from 1995 to 2004.

A regular on *The Caroline Rhea Show*, Dulcy also wrote and produced for this series, and developed her own comedy segments. Her credits also include pilots for CBS and NBC, namely *Boy Meets Girl* and *The World According to Noah*. As a teenager, Dulcy started in theatre at the Westport Country Playhouse, where she returned in 1998 to co-star with Bader, sister Amanda and her husband Frank Ferrante, and parents June and David Rogers for *The Perfect Wedding*.

DULCY ROGERS and real-life husband Diedrich Bader
The Drew Carey Show.

Comedy

RCA Victor 8PT 7030 (1956).

Christopher Lloyd

The cast of the sitcom *Taxi* became TV favorites — and stars — during its 1978-83 run. Among them, CHRISTOPHER LLOYD, gave a memorable portrayal as the spaced-out ex-hippie Reverend Jim, and picked up Emmys back to back in 1982-83. In 1992 for the lead in a drama series *Avonlea* on the Disney Channel, he received his third Emmy.

This Staples High School grad also worked in films, most notably as Doc in the *Back to the Future* trilogy and in *The Addams Family* and its sequel. In 1995 he returned to TV in the series *Deadly Games*. Lloyd stood out as the evil super-villain Sebastian Jackal, a character unleashed from a video game. This wild comedy-adventure co-starred another Westport performer, Cindy Gibb. Lloyd then played another science-whiz Doc in the TNT movie *The Big Time*, about the formative days of television.

A prolific character actor, he's been seen on *Malcolm in the Middle*, *Law & Order: Criminal Intent*, *The West Wing*, *Meteor* and *Knights of Bloodsteel* since 2004.

CHRISTOPHER LLOYD with *Taxi* regulars: Tony Danza, Andy Kaufman, Carol Kane, Danny DeVito, Judd Hirsch, Marilu Henner (1979-1983).

Patricia Englund

PATRICIA ENGLUND enlivened the news and political satire *That Was The Week That Was* in the turbulent mid-1960s. The NBC series began as a special in late 1963 and premiered as a "live" — and lively — weekly show the following January. Elliott Reid was the original host, followed by David Frost who had hosted the British version. Pat often teamed up with Phyllis Newman and Nancy Ames for skits aimed at such topics as civil rights, religion and politicians (Barry Goldwater was a frequent target).

Englund had honed her talent with the acclaimed improvisation theatre company, Second City. She was seen regularly on the NBC series *For Richer, For Poorer*, and made her daytime bow in 1977 on *Friends and Lovers*. She also served as a NBC weather girl.

The daughter of actress Mabel Albertson, Pat worked on Broadway with Katharine Hepburn and Bert Lahr, and as Ado Annie in *Oklahoma!* A native Californian, she settled in Westport many years ago for what she called a "more regular life."

PATRICIA ENGLUND on *That Was The Week That Was* (1964).

Joan Blondell

By the time JOAN BLONDELL (1909-1979) ventured into television, her programs were competing with telecasts of her many films of the 1930s and '40s. On screen often as a wisecracking chorine, she also had a big following from dramas (*A Tree Grows in Brooklyn*) and musicals (*Footlight Parade*).

Blondell's first major TV series *Here Come The Brides*, a comedy adventure, aired from 1968 to 1970. Earlier, in 1963, she had briefly appeared on *The Real McCoys* with Walter Brennan. In the '70s she played Peggy Revere, whose secretarial school provided private-eye Miles Banyon (Robert Forster) with a new secretary each week. Her acting career spanned a half-century, and midway in the 1950s, she settled on Westport's Bayberry Lane with her two children and a boxer dog Booker.

During an early TV guest appearance — on ABC's celebrity-filled *Penthouse Party* hosted by Betty Furness — Joan revealed an unexpected talent by whipping up a casserole in short order.

JOAN BLONDELL and her son Norman Powell, director of *The New Dick Van Dyke Show* (1973).

Barbara Rhoades

While a dancer on Broadway in *Funny Girl*, BARBARA RHOADES took a screen test at Universal. The studio signed her for films (*Don't Just Stand There, Shakiest Gun in the West*). TV roles — primarily comedy and mystery — began in 1968. She played an escort service girl, Melody, the statuesque next-door neighbor of young grad Lenny (Adam Arkin) in *Busting Loose* at CBS. Barbara appeared on *The Blue Knight* with George Kennedy, *Joe Forrester* starring Lloyd Bridges and *You Again?* opposite Jack Klugman. As private detective Maggie Chandler, she was part of the large cast of the controversial satire *Soap* in its last season, 1980-81.

At CBS Barbara coached the women's team for the 1978 *Celebrity Challenge of the Sexes*. More recently she was on an episode of *Law & Order*.

Barbara and her husband, writer-producer Bernie Orenstein, looked for a retirement area near family and New York in 1995. They checked out Weston, especially its schools for their young son, and opted for that community

Madeline Kahn

The 1970 CBS series *Comedy Tonight* led actress-singer MADELINE KAHN (1942-1999) to a notable career in films (*Paper Moon, Blazing Saddles, What's Up Doc?*) and roles on Broadway (*Promenade, Two by Two*).

She returned to TV in the 1980s with her own short-lived show *Oh Madeline*, a sitcom heavy with slapstick. Kahn is warmly remembered as the eccentric best friend Pauline on *Cosby* (1996-99).

A former Weston resident, she played in the series *Mr. President* with George C. Scott and in *New York News* opposite Gregory Harrison. On Broadway, Kahn won a Tony for *The Sisters Rosenweig* in 1993.

MADELINE KAHN did *Cosby* with Bill Cosby and Phylicia Rashad (1996-1999).

Brett Somers

A new generation of game show fans has encountered wisecracking celebrity panelist BRETT SOMERS (1924-2007) from frequent reruns on cable of *The Match Game*. The contestants won if their answers to double-entendre nonsense questions asked by host Gene Rayburn matched those of the six-member panel, chiefly Brett, Charles Nelson Reilly, Betty White and Dick Martin, during the quiz's 1975-1982 telecasts.

Brett, a talented and popular participant in Westport's Theatre Artists Workshop, began her career playing in early live TV dramas and with comedian Jack Carter. She went on to guest appearances in such series as *The Love Boat* and *The Mary Tyler Moore Show*. On *Perry Mason* she did a season as the character Gertrude Lade.

For *The Odd Couple*, she played Oscar's ex-wife, Blanche. In the role of Oscar was her real-life husband, Jack Klugman. The ABC sitcom ran for 13 years, beginning in 1970.

BRETT SOMERS marries Jack Klugman, with Tony Randall as Best Man, on *The Odd Couple* flashback episode (1973).

Phyllis Newman

Versatile PHYLLIS NEWMAN presented one-woman musical shows and additional theatre credits beginning in the 1950s, going on to win the 1962 Tony for best featured actress in *Subways are for Sleeping*. CBS provided her with leads in the detective drama *Diagnosis: Unknown* and the sitcom *Coming of Age*.

Yet it was a TV lampoon of people and events in the news called *That Was The Week That Was* (1964-65) at NBC that allowed her to combine comedy sketches, songs and dance in a memorable satirical mix. The show attracted much attention and large audiences for its irreverent brand of humor.

Newman also became a regular on *To Tell the Truth* and *What's My Line?*, and on *100 Centre Street*. She appeared on the *Tonight* and *Ed Sullivan* shows. In 1960 Phyllis married Broadway and film lyricist Adolph Green, and when not in Manhattan, they chose Westport for their country place.

Her bout with cancer led to founding the Phyllis Newman Women's Health Initiative of The Actors' Fund, and to her hosting the annual "Nothing Like a Dame" galas which have served 2,500 women in the entertainment industry. In 2009 Phyllis received a special Tony for her humanitarian work.

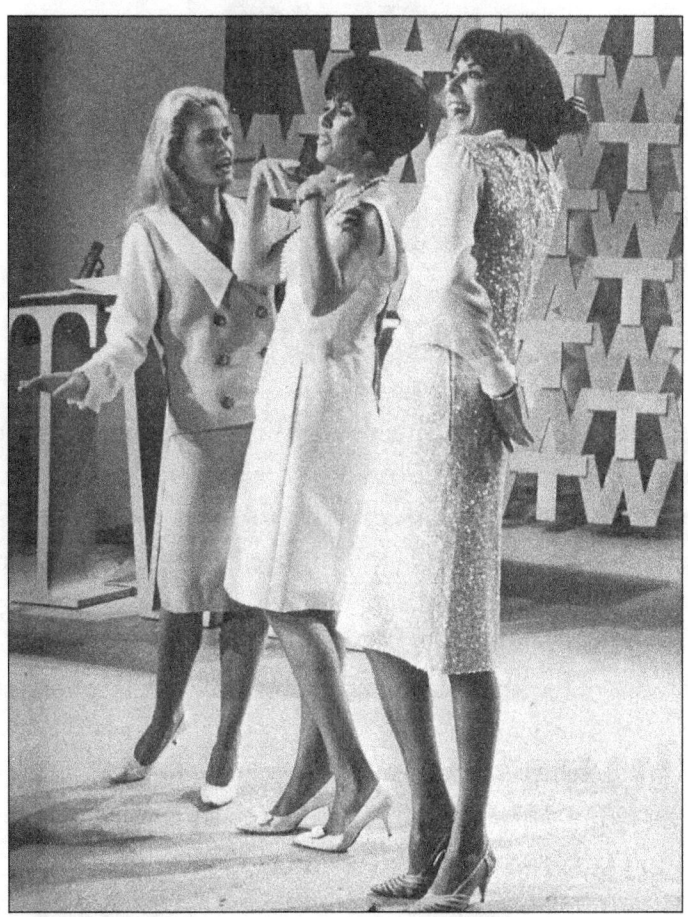

PHYLLIS NEWMAN (center), Nancy Ames, Pat Englund recap *That Was The Week That Was* (1964-1965).

Marlo Thomas

Best known for her starring role in the independent woman series *That Girl*, MARLO THOMAS in the 1960s started a trend for single, urban career-girl comedies that followed with those of Mary Tyler Moore and Doris Day. Thomas played Ann who came to New York to pursue acting, and on the first telecast met magazine executive Don Hollinger (Ted Bessell), her first romance. Marlo also produced the series. Earlier, she portrayed Stella for one season on *The Joey Bishop Show*.

Thomas created, produced and co-hosted the children's special *Free to Be.... You and Me*, which received Emmy and Peabody Awards in 1974, and that subsequently became a best-selling book and record. A follow-up presentation, *Free to Be.... a Family*, won the Emmy in 1989. Another Emmy, as Best Dramatic Actress for *Nobody's Child*, was presented to her in 1986.

More recently, Marlo guest-starred as Jennifer Aniston's mother on *Friends*, an Emmy-nominated role. The daughter of actor Danny Thomas, she was a long-time resident of the Greens Farms section of Westport with husband Phil Donahue, whom she married in 1980.

MARLO THOMAS as *That Girl*, prototype for "independent woman" series (1966-1971).

Martha Raye

Knockabout comedy mixed with rowdy songs carried MARTHA RAYE (1916-1994) from movies to television stardom. One of the earliest film comediennes to host a variety series, she brought vaudeville to TV with *All Star Revue* in 1951-53, then headlined her own comedy hour, *The Martha Raye Show*.

By the next decade, her career slumped. In 1976 Rock Hudson brought her back to TV as his jocular housekeeper on *McMillan and Wife*. That led to *The Love Boat* appearances and *Alice*, as Mel's mother, from 1982-84, and then to spokesperson for Polident.

With most early variety shows based in New York, Raye settled in Westport, commuting regularly to the City. On the train trip home, she often turned the club car into a full-fledged party causing commuters occasionally to over-shoot their destinations, ending up at stations beyond Westport.

MARTHA RAYE, Mel's mother on *Alice*, with Vic Tayback (1982-1984).

Mabel Albertson

Contributing sharply-honed character performances on stage and film, MABEL ALBERTSON (1901-1982) hit her stride on TV as judgmental, wisecracking mothers and mothers-in-law. From the 1950s cast of *That's My Boy* led by comedian Eddie Mayehoff and *Those Whiting Girls* costarring sisters Margaret and Barbara Whiting, Mabel soon became a regular as Grandma Brady on the *Tom Ewell Show* and Mrs. Hollinger on Marlo Thomas's *That Girl*.

Bewitched provided a role in a comedy that's often seen on reruns. Albertson appeared in that extremely popular sitcom as Phyllis Stephens, Samantha's mother-in-law. The series took place in Westport, and when it ended in 1972, the veteran actress moved east to a house in Westport, and near her daughter, actress Patricia Englund.

MABEL ALBERTSON, Roy Roberts as Mr. & Mrs. Stephens on *Bewitched*.

Eva Gabor

The youngest of the glamorous, much-married Gabor sisters, EVA GABOR (1921-1995) proved to be an actress beyond mere celebrity status. The 1950 Broadway play *The Happy Time* won her critical praise and led to guest TV roles on *Tales of Tomorrow, Ponds Theatre, Suspense* and several variety shows. Then came her own interview program *The Eva Gabor Show*.

Her best-known role was as an out-of-place Park Avenue socialite on a run-down farm on *Green Acres* (1965-71). She played the fashionable city dweller opposite Eddie Albert's farm-loving husband on this high-rated CBS rural comedy. And it gave her stardom independent of the daffy Gabor family image.

Hungarian-born Eva returned to TV as a Washington socialite in the 1986 series *Bridges to Cross*. She did many stage roles (*Blithe Spirit, Private Lives*) and several memorable movies (*The Last Time I Saw Paris, Gigi*). She starred in *Return to Green Acres*, a made-for-TV movie in 1990.

The onetime Westport resident, who was married four times, was credited with saying, "Marriage is too interesting an experiment to be tried only once or twice."

EVA GABOR as Lisa, Eddie Albert as Oliver, *Green Acres* (1965-1971).

Imogene Coca

Partner in one of TV's most successful comedy teams, IMOGENE COCA (1908-2001) began as a singer-dancer in nightclubs. She was hailed as a new Broadway comedienne for her routines with young Henry Fonda in *New Faces of 1934*. However, she was often out of work until her TV career began in 1949. Then, it was rags to riches: $10,000 a week! 1949's *Admiral Broadway Revue* united Coca with funnyman Sid Caesar. Telecast "live" from the newly built International Theatre in New York, the program featured a half-dozen comedy skits and aired simultaneously over both the DuMont and NBC networks. It was a forerunner of NBC's *Your Show of Shows*, which reached 25 million people on Saturday nights from 1950-54. Imogene's talents as a pantomime delighted audiences the most. Her own sitcom, *The Imogene Coca Show*, followed for the 1954-55 season.

The second actress to win an Emmy (1952), she reteamed with Caesar for *The Sid Caesar-Imogene Coca-Carl Reiner-Howard Morris Show*, a special that picked up Emmys in 1967. Other prestigious awards and TV appearances on *Bewitched*, *Moonlighting* and *One Life to Live* followed. Before her retirement to Westport in the 1990s, she toured the country with Caesar in a version of *Your Show of Shows*. Imogene Coca lives on in late-night kinescope re-runs of this TV classic.

IMOGENE COCA and co-stars Sid Caesar, Carl Reiner, Howard Morris, *Your Show of Shows* (1950-1954).

Kerri Kenney-Silver

Actress-musician-writer KERRI KENNEY-SILVER bowed in 1994 with *The State*, a sketch comedy show on MTV. She also wrote for the series, and later filled similar roles for *Viva Variety* over Comedy Central. A lampoon on TV variety programs, it featured Kenney-Silver as Agatha Laupin with co-host Thomas Lennon (as the slick but inept Mr. Laupin). For that network, she also found success in *Reno 911!*, a police parody.

In 2001 the Westport-born performer was Pam on *The Ellen Show* and the voice of Tish's mom for the Disney cartoon *The Weekenders* on Family Channel. Kerri also was a member of the all-female rock group called Cake Like. Her father Larry Kenney is known for his classic voice-over work.

KERRI KENNEY, Thomas Lennon, Michael Ian Black, *Viva Variety* (1997-1998).

Frank Gorshin

No matter whether it was film, television, nightclub or stage, FRANK GORSHIN (1934-2005) was readily available for work. He moved from one segment of show business to another as a character actor and impressionist. B-movies (*Hot Rod Girl, Invasion of the Saucer Men*) to Broadway (*Jimmy* as NY Mayor Jimmy Walker; *Say Goodnight, Gracie* as comic George Burns) to TV (episodes of *Star Trek* and *Edge of Night*), Gorshin was a cult fan favorite.

Above all, he's remembered for the 1960s camp TV series *Batman*. "Riddle me this," he'd growl in this fantasy adventure, an overnight sensation airing two-part stories that ran two nights a week on ABC. Gorshin repeated his colorful role as the dastardly villain in the *Batman* movie version.

In the 1980s he camped out in an 18-room Westport home on Cross Highway, a long way from his youthful days as an usher in a Pittsburgh theatre where he watched movie stars and began impersonating such favorites as Cagney, Brando and Bogart.

FRANK GORSHIN as "The Riddler," *Batman* (1966-1967).

Kipp Marcus

At age 14 KIPP MARCUS tried out for a Broadway revival of *Oliver!* — and got a part. It quickly led to his second professional audition, to play Beaver's son Kip on *The New Leave It to Beaver* TV series in 1985. Kipp commuted from Staples High School to LA for 100 episodes, a sequel to the 1950s sitcom of the Cleaver family.

Marcus's teen years also saw the beginning of a writing career that won him a Young Playwrights of Connecticut Award for Best Play. He's written and produced several films, directed by his brother, Adam Marcus, including *Let It Snow*, a comedy shot in Westport. A selection at the 2000 Sundance Film Festival, it was soon on HBO.

An acting honors graduate of NYU's Tisch School of the Arts, Kipp performed the roles of Marius and Jean Prouvaire in the tenth anniversary Broadway production of *Les Miserables*.

KIPP MARCUS joined the Cleaver family for the Beaver sequel in the 1980s.

David Groh

"Rhoda's Wedding" was one of the highest-rated sitcom episodes on TV. Her bridegroom, Joe, gave DAVID GROH (1939-2008) his best role on a series. Rhoda and Joe were wed in a full-hour telecast in 1974, but after two years of marriage, the producers decided to separate the couple and head them toward divorce. Groh was gradually phased out. Single again, Rhoda Morgenstern, played by Valerie Harper, lasted only one more season on CBS.

Groh's post-*Rhoda* TV credits include the soap *General Hospital* and sitcom *Another Day*. His episodic appearances ran the gamut from *Police Story* and *Murder, She Wrote* to *Sisters* and *Melrose Place*. He was often seen in TV movies, such as *Victory at Entebbe* (1976) and *Take My Advice: The Ann and Abby Story* (1999).

A Fulbright scholar following graduation from Brown, Groh appeared on stage in *Antony and Cleopatra* and *Chapter Two*.

DAVID GROH played husband Joe to Valerie Harper's *Rhoda* (1974-1977).

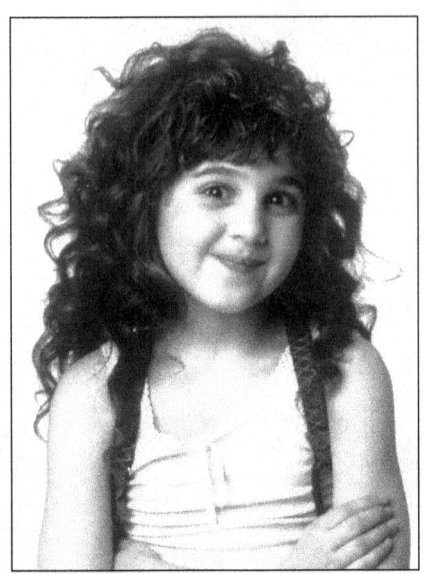

Alisan Porter

Ed McMahon's *Star Search* first discovered young singer ALISAN PORTER at age five. She became the youngest participant ever to win on that show. It led to *Pee-Wee's Playhouse*, the miniseries *I'll Take Manhattan* and the sitcom *Chicken Soup*. In 1991 Alisan played the lead in the film *Curly Sue*.

When she was 18, she moved from Westport to New York for Broadway shows, including *Footloose* and a revival of *A Chorus Line*.

Actress, singer and dancer, she performed for The Raz, and then with her band, The Alisan Porter Project.

While living in Westport, he co-starred in *Doubles* at the Westport Country Playhouse in the 1980s.

Soaps

Admiral 19A11 (1948)

Ed Bryce

ED BRYCE (1921-1999) "became" Bill Bauer from a dozen years of Monday-thru-Friday telecasts of the soap *Guiding Light*. A standout in the dramatic role of the Bauer family's son Bill, a womanizer and drifter, Ed's character had the first heart transplant on daytime TV (1969). When the hospital scene was over, he didn't get up. There was momentary concern until he opened his eyes. Ed had simply fallen fast asleep on the operating table!

Bryce was long familiar with "live" programs, and quick costume and set changes, usually during commercial breaks.

An early series of his called *Captain Applejack* focused on a timid husband who in his dreams became a swashbuckling pirate; the living room scene was at one end of the studio, the pirate ship at the other — and one camera in the middle of the floor. The year was 1948, and Ed had just won the Theatre World Award for the lead in Broadway's *The Cradle Will Rock*.

He also made his mark on TV as Captain Strong on *Tom Corbett, Space Cadet*, an early 1950s children's science-fiction series that was simulcast over ABC radio. It is now a cult classic.

Ed Bryce and his wife Dorothy raised three sons in Westport, where both contributed to all aspects of the performing arts, from acting and singing to writing, teaching and directing.

ED BRYCE as Bill Bauer on *The Guiding Light*, with actress Charita Bauer.

Scott Bryce

One of the first soaps to expand from 15 minutes to a half hour, *As The World Turns* provided the training ground for numerous future headliners: Richard Thomas, Julianne Moore, Martin Sheen, Meg Ryan, and SCOTT BRYCE. Beginning in 1982, Scott, as Craig Montgomery, fell in love with Meg Ryan's character, Betsy, and was determined not to let anyone have her if he couldn't possess her. His role continued for five years, and he then made several reappearances on the show over the years until 2008.

Acting since his high-school days in Westport, Scott is active in television with primetime guest appearances on *ER*, *Law & Order*, *Reba* and *Judging Amy*. He starred on the serial drama *2000 Malibu Road*, and appeared in several Movies of the Week for CBS. For the sitcom *Murphy Brown*, he played Will Forrest who married and later divorced Corky (Faith Ford).

For several seasons, starting in 1999, he was the lead in the series *Popular*, and appeared on *One Life to Live* in 2006-07. Scott is executive producer at the New Palace Digital Studio in Norwalk where his Rabbit Ears Entertainment produces children's books on DVD, one of which features Meryl Streep.

SCOTT BRYCE and cast of *Popular* (2001).

Kevin Conroy

Westport native KEVIN CONROY has performed in numerous Shakespeare plays in companies and festivals throughout the country, and made his Broadway debut in Edward Albee's *Lolita*. His principal TV appearances began with *Another World*, followed by another soap, *Search for Tomorrow*, as Chase Kendall.

Bearing a striking resemblance to young Teddy Kennedy, Kevin was cast as the Massachusetts senator in the 1983 miniseries *Kennedy*. Other TV credits for the Juilliard-trained actor include *Dynasty*, *Tour of Duty*, *Rachel Gunn, RN*, and the miniseries *George Washington*.

He is best known for his voice role as Batman in numerous animated TV series, films and video games. Conroy has portrayed the superhero longer than any other actor in either live-action or animation.

KEVIN CONROY and Susan Carey-Lamm, *Search for Tomorrow*.

William Prince

WILLIAM PRINCE (1913-1996) acted on tour and Broadway in Shakespearean roles and the works of Eugene O'Neill, Edward Albee and Maxwell Anderson. He was first noticed by audiences after Eva Le Gallienne, responding to his plea for an audition, gave him a part in *Ah, Wilderness!* in the 1940s. Warner Bros. soon brought him to Hollywood for work in *Objective, Burma!*, *Cinderella Jones* and *Pillow to Post*. That led to the role of Christian in *Cyrano de Bergerac* in 1950.

Back on stage, he played Christopher Isherwood opposite Julie Harris in *I am a Camera*.

Numerous TV appearances followed. He commuted from Westport to New York for the crime/law dramas *The Mask* and *Justice*, and for the title role on *Young Doctor Malone* for five years. His wife, actress Augusta Dabney, was featured with him on this long-running radio-to-TV crossover.

WILLIAM PRINCE (lower left) in lead role, *Young Doctor Malone* with John Connell, Freda Holloway, Augusta Dabney (1958-1963).

Larry Haines

A veteran of some 15,000 radio broadcasts, LARRY HAINES (1918-2008) played on television's first soap opera, *The First Hundred Years*, in the early 1950s. He soon auditioned for the part as Stu Bergman on CBS daytime's *Search for Tomorrow*, a role that was his for 35 years. He won two Emmys (1976 and 1980) as outstanding actor in this series.

Haines made guest appearances on *Maude*, *Kojak* and *The Defenders*, and co-starred in *Phyl and Mikky*. In 1983 he received the TV Academy's Lifetime Achievement Award.

On Broadway he appeared in *Tribute*, *A Thousand Clowns*, and gained Tony nominations for *Promises, Promises* and *Generation*. His movies include *The Odd Couple* and *The Swimmer* with Burt Lancaster, which was filmed in 1968 at swimming pools near the Haines home in Weston.

He retired to Delray Beach, Florida in the 1990s.

LARRY HAINES, Melba Rae, Mary Stuart celebrate, *Search for Tomorrow*.

Mary Stuart

On September 3, 1951, the future "Queen of Soaps" — MARY STUART (1925-2002) — began her *Search for Tomorrow*. Bowing on that then-15-minute "live" CBS series as the kind, thoughtful and loving wife Joanne Barron, she performed that role day after day, year after year, until 1986. The top-rated show, aired from New York, was sponsored by Proctor & Gamble, whose venerable products, Joy and Spic and Span, were introduced on its premiere.

Stuart was the first daytime actress to have her pregnancy written into the plot. The producers even filmed her at the hospital after she gave birth to her son in 1956. In 1963 she was nominated for an Emmy for Best Actress in a Continued Series. She later received a Lifetime Achievement Emmy Award. Stuart also played Meta Brown on *The Guiding Light*. A singer and composer, she pursued an acting career in Hollywood in the 1940s, appearing on screen with Ronald Reagan and Errol Flynn.

In 1960 Stuart bought a cottage in Weston on three acres. In her autobiography, *Both of Me*, she describes this weekend retreat as "a perfect place to enjoy the sun in the morning and a martini at eventide."

MARY STUART (seated) played Jo, pivotal character on *Search for Tomorrow* (1951-1986).

Frank Runyeon

Voted one of the three most popular leading men on daytime TV four years straight in the 1980s, FRANK RUNYEON pursued a soap opera career that is well remembered by fans. In his TV heyday he shared star billing with Meg Ryan on *As The World Turns* and portrayed defrocked priest Father Donnelly in *Santa Barbara*. There were periodic guest shots on *Falcon Crest, General Hospital* and *LA Law*, along with a run on *Another World*.

A Princeton graduate and piano student at Juilliard, Runyeon, after a decade in the limelight, gradually withdrew from the TV world into a soul-searching phase. Settling in Westport in 1992, he enrolled in divinity school. He learned Greek to translate the Gospel of St. Mark into a one-man play spoken in everyday language. Titled *Afraid!* it has become a highly praised production, seen at churches, theatres and universities across America.

Frank decided to pursue his doctorate in Biblical studies in lieu of becoming an Episcopal priest.

FRANK RUNYEON and Meg Ryan on *As The World Turns* (1982).

Martin West

The TV acting credits of MARTIN WEST span more than 30 years including notable guest appearances on *Hill Street Blues*. On daytime shows, he played Don Hughes on *As The World Turns* for two years and Phil Brewer on *General Hospital* for seven years in Los Angeles. There, he also made films for Alfred Hitchcock (*Family Plot*) and John Carpenter (*Assault on Thirteenth Precinct*), and was a founding member of the West Coast's most prestigious theatrical workshop, Theatre East, where he directed and produced plays.

Martin settled in Westport in the 1990s, not long after he started a production company creating documentaries, TV programs and promotions for the entertainment industry. Locally, he directed and produced the Annual Arts Awards starting in 1998-99, which have aired on Connecticut Public Television.

His film *Gathering of Glory*, about the unique history of the arts in Westport and Weston, premiered in September 2003. His 2009 documentary *Years in the Making: A Journey into Late Life Creativity* features 50 local visual artists over the age of 70 still actively producing their works.

MARTIN WEST, with Diana Maynard, played Phil Brewer on *General Hospital* for seven years.

Victoria Wyndham

For 27 years, until the soap's cancellation in 1999, VICTORIA WYNDHAM played Rachel Cory on *Another World*. In addition to Rachel, she portrayed Justine Kirkland on this program. She has been a three-time Emmy nominee and winner of the 1978 *Soap Opera Digest* award for best actress. She made her daytime debut on *Guiding Light* in 1967.

Wyndham began her career in Broadway's *Fiddler on the Roof*, and performed for two years with Lily Tomlin in a satirical and improvisational revue.

She has created librettos, directed dance specials and produced and directed rock bands in both video and recording formats. Raised in Westport, Victoria is the daughter of the late actor Ralph Camargo.

VICTORIA WYNDHAM marries Douglas Watson on *Another World* with real-life father actor Ralph Camargo officiating

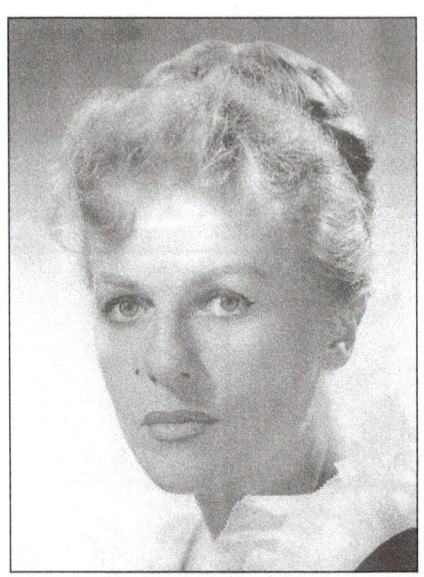

Lisa Chapman

An original cast member in 1964 of NBC's *Another World*, LISA CHAPMAN (1929-1967) played nonconformist Janet Mathews until, two years later in real life, she became pregnant with her fourth child. Alas, her "soap character" wasn't able to have children, so she was dropped from the series. Before her untimely death at age 37, Lisa also appeared in several episodes of *The Secret Storm*.

A graduate of Yale Drama School, she worked for Eva Le Gallienne at the White Barn Theatre, where she portrayed Regina in Ibsen's *Ghosts*. In New York she appeared in an Equity Library production of *Lysistrata* and on TV's *Home Show*.

Chapman and her husband, the concert pianist and conductor Andrew Heath, settled in Westport in the late 1950s, and she did much for the community as a volunteer at the Westport Woman's Club, Assumption Church and Fairfield University. Her TV work usually entailed a 6 a.m. train ride to the city and NBC studios, where the cast rehearsed, then aired the show live at 3 p.m. "Then we get a new script. I study it and usually it's bed by 9 at night to be ready for the next day's airing."

Haila Stoddard

Actress, writer and producer HAILA STODDARD took center stage in the 1930s when she toured the U.S. for 15 months as Pearl in the classic *Tobacco Road*, before a New York bow in *Yes, My Darling Daughter*. Hardly a year passed without Haila on Broadway, on tour and in summer stock, or as producer-director.

In 1954 she assumed the role of Pauline Harris on the TV soap *Secret Storm*, beginning a 16-year run! This Weston resident also did more than 100 teleplays on *Playhouse 90*, *Studio One* and *Hallmark Hall of Fame*. She adapted the works of James Thurber for an acclaimed TV series in 1965. Haila is the widow of actor Whit Connor.

HAILA STODDARD as Pauline Harris on *The Secret Storm*, with Peter Hobbs (1954-1970).

Whit Connor

WHIT CONNOR (1916-1988) began his acting career on radio with a role on *The Lone Ranger*. Following WWII military duty, he appeared on Broadway in *Hamlet* and *Macbeth*, winning a Theatre World award in 1948, the same year he entered films with *Tap Roots*.

Connor was seen on TV's *Omnibus*, *Studio One* and *The Guiding Light*. For the 1954-55 season he co-starred with June Havoc on the CBS sitcom *Willy*. He played a veterinarian in a small New Hampshire town and the boyfriend of Havoc.

A mainstay of stock and summer theatre, he married actress-producer Haila Stoddard in 1956, and they lived in Weston.

WHIT CONNOR, Zina Bethune, *The Guiding Light*.

Bobra Suiter

BOBRA SUITER owned the established role of head nurse Barbara at Cedars Hospital on *Guiding Light* for 17 years. And she also played small parts in *Another World* and *As the World Turns* such as portraying a prison matron or sanitarium inmate.

Starting out in radio in the Midwest, she was hired by Richard Rodgers for his Broadway show *Carousel*. Then came *Brigadoon* and *Kiss Me Kate*, followed by roles in the films *Marathon Man* and *Trading Places*.

Bobra came to Westport in 1968, shortly after her husband joined the Famous Artists School as an administrator. Recent prime-time TV credits include *The Adams Chronicles* and *Saturday Night Live*.

Music & Dance

Philco Predicta UG-3412 Siesta (1959).

Cindy Gibb

Starting ballet lessons at age five from her mother Linde at the Westport Dance Center, CINDY GIBB was modeling and acting by her teens. Woody Allen tapped her for a part in *Stardust Memories* at 17. But she has built a career through TV films, including *Gypsy* (as young June Havoc) and the title role in *The Karen Carpenter Story*.

Cindy also appeared in the soap *Search for Tomorrow* and as Holly Laird for three seasons in the musical drama *Fame*, beginning on syndication in 1983. She played magazine editor Meg, daughter (and boss) of columnist Jack Buckner (Dabney Coleman) in the sitcom *Madman of The People*, and Lauren, ex-wife of video enthusiast Gus (James Calvert), in the sci-fi series *Deadly Games*.

CYNTHIA GIBB (center), leading dancer on *Fame* (1983-1986).

Eartha Kitt

Singer, actress and dancer EARTHA KITT (1927-2008) won early fame on Broadway with *New Faces of 1952* and *Mrs. Patterson*. Her nightclub, film appearances and recordings featured her sultry and haunting vocal renditions of "C'est Si Bon," "Santa Baby" and dozens of other songs.

Episodic television appearances range from *Omnibus* and *Playhouse 90* to *I Spy* and *Miami Vice*. Then Kitt made a lasting impression as the Catwoman on *Batman*, the ultimate TV "camp" show of the 1960s and based on the comic-book adventures.

In 1996 she received an Image Award nomination for outstanding supporting actress in a comedy series *Living Single*. Eartha settled in Weston to be near her daughter, Kitt Shapiro, who managed her tours and recording activities.

EARTHA KITT, "Catwoman," *Batman* (1967-1968).

James Melton

The concert hall, recording and radio studio, and opera house; JAMES MELTON (1904-1961) mastered them all. His success made it clear that when network TV linked both coasts, this medium would be his next in an outstanding singing career.

In 1951 Ford Motor signed Jimmy as tenor-emcee for *Ford Festival*, an hour-long musical variety series on NBC. But concert-type programs never caught on in competition with sitcoms, dramatic presentations and sports events. Melton lasted only a season, faring not much better (or worse) than many crossover singers from primetime radio.

An avid yachtsman, Melton anchored his 64-foot cruiser at Westport in 1937, and settled into a pre-Revolutionary farmhouse in Weston. He was widely known as a collector of vintage autos, owning 82 vehicles that he displayed in a museum on Route 7 in Norwalk. In the 1940s he was a common sight driving them on local roads, and he served on the Merritt Parkway commission.

JAMES MELTON at the wheel of an antique automobile from his large Connecticut collection.

Bambi Lynn and Rod Alexander

Early television's top dance team met (and married) while both were on Broadway in *It's Great to Be Alive* in 1950. BAMBI LYNN and ROD ALEXANDER (1922-1992) worked up an act for nightclubs, and then were signed for TV's *Show of Shows* on which they appeared with Sid Caesar and Imogene Coca for two and a half years. They later went on to dance on major musical programs, including the Ed Sullivan, Steve Allen and Andy Williams shows.

Bambi studied ballet before dancing lead roles in the 1940s Broadway hits *Oklahoma!* and *Carousel*, and playing Alice in *Alice in Wonderland* with Eva Le Gallienne. She made her film debut as the "Dream Ballet" Laurie in *Oklahoma!*

Rod Alexander studied and worked with Jack Cole, dancing jazz, modern and tap. He choreographed countless routines for such TV shows as *Arthur Murray Party, Arthur Godfrey's Talent Scouts* and Max Liebman spectaculars. "The home screen," he observed, "has made millions of additional fans for a wide variety of dance."

Rod and Bambi settled in Westport in the late 1950s, shortly before they divorced. Bambi opened a dance studio on South Compo Road with her second husband, Joseph De Jesus. In the 1980s she worked as a dance critic for the *Westport News* and today often leaves her Florida home for acting jobs and to lecture on choreography in schools and colleges.

BAMBI LYNN and ROD ALEXANDER, *Your Show of Shows* (1952-1954).

Neil Sedaka

While still a teenager NEIL SEDAKA wrote the pop hit "Stupid Cupid" for Connie Francis, and followed up with a string of best-selling songs, including "Oh, Carole," "Breaking Up Is Hard To Do" and "Happy Birthday, Sweet Sixteen." In 1961 he began to record his own compositions, accumulating a handful of gold albums.

A Juilliard-trained classical pianist, he made his television debut on *The Dick Clark Saturday Night Show*, opening by playing Chopin and closing with "I Go Ape." Sedaka appeared on the 1960s *Shindig*, one of the first rock 'n' roll sessions on TV. His guest appearances boosted ratings for *On Stage, America* and *You Write the Songs*. In 1976 he starred in his own NBC special, featuring his vintage songs and newer tunes — "oldies and goodies," as he describes them.

Neil and his family lived at 14 East Meadow Road in Westport for many years, in a home owned at previous times by both Martha Raye and David Wayne.

NEIL SEDAKA, piano prodigy-songwriter, made his TV debut on *Dick Clark Saturday Night Show.*

Fritz Reiner

One of the foremost 20th-century symphony conductors, along with Toscanini and Stokowski, Hungarian-born FRITZ REINER (1888-1963) made his debut at 21 directing *Carmen* at the Budapest Opera. He came to America in the 1920s, taking the podium of the Cincinnati Orchestra. A decade later, Reiner led the Pittsburgh Symphony, and made frequent guest appearances with other world-class companies, including the Met Opera, Covent Garden and San Francisco Symphony.

Recordings and radio added to his distinguished career. Shortly after becoming leader of the Chicago Symphony, he was engaged for a weekly DuMont TV series with that orchestra, first telecast in January 1954. This classical music program also provided commentary about the composers and their works, and ran until April 1955.

Off-season, Reiner and his actress wife Carlotta Irwin spent time at "Rambleside," their home in Weston.

FRITZ REINER studies scores for 1954-55 Chicago Symphony TV series.

Hosts

Panther on Delco TV-71 (1948).

Don Imus

Talk-show host DON IMUS broadcast five days a week during morning drive time. *Imus in the Morning* at its peak was syndicated to over 90 radio markets coast to coast, and in 1996 became simulcast via MSNBC cable. But the outrage from an insensitive and ill-conceived remark characterizing the Rutger University women's basketball team as "hos" led to immediate suspension from the airwaves. Imus apologized for his offensive words. His absence lasted a year until WABC radio and RED-TV brought him back to the air.

In 2009 he joined Fox Business Channel for his three-hour morning program, described as "current events, political humor and satire with a roster of high-profile newsmakers." Imus continues to attract legions of listeners and viewers.

His early jobs ranged from railroad brakeman and copper miner to U.S. Marine and rock band leader. He connected with radio as a DJ in California in 1968, then moved on to Cleveland, and in 1971 to New York's WNBC. He has used his show to raise millions of dollars to benefit children's charities, including those addressing pediatric cancer and sudden infant death syndrome. In 1997 *Time* magazine called him a most influential American.

Preferring life on his cattle ranch in New Mexico, Imus often spent weekends at his Westport property looking out over Long Island Sound.

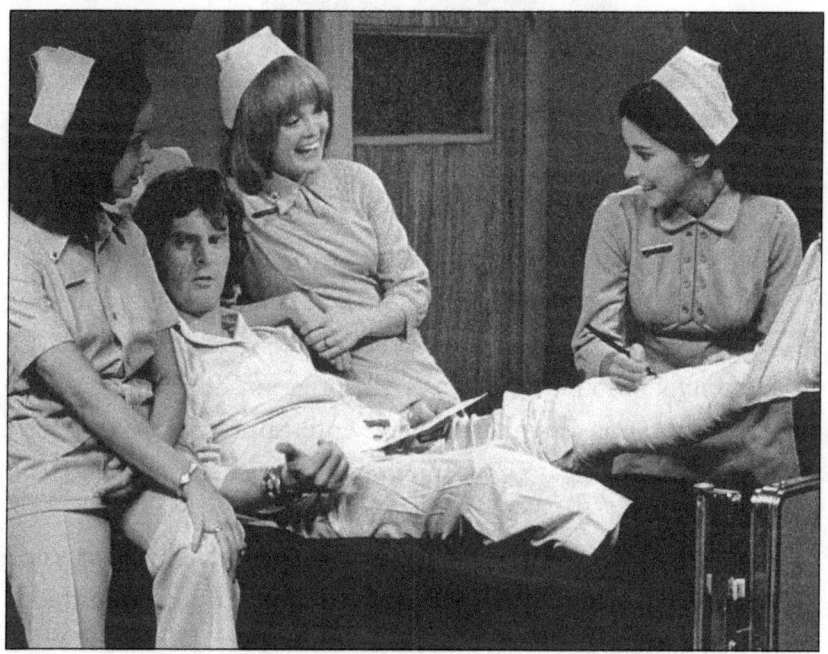

DON IMUS is welcomed as a guest on *The Doctors*.

David Susskind

A crusader for better drama on television and more mature and intelligent programming, DAVID SUSSKIND (1920-1987) started in 1946 as a press and talent agent. His first clients included leading TV producers, directors and writers.

He briefly switched to MCA's TV program department to sell programs to sponsors and manage entertainers. Susskind soon turned to producing *Philco Television Playhouse, Armstrong Circle Theatre* and other TV, screen and stage dramas.

In New York in 1958 he began his own weekly discussion program, *Open End*, often with remote pickups and roundtable talks with guests. He made headlines when he had Soviet Premier Khrushchev for an interview in 1960. His company, Talent Associates, Ltd., by 1960 had also produced 26 plays on the prestigious *Play of the Week*, a Peabody Award winner.

Susskind picked up a handful of Emmys, beginning as co-producer of the CBS program *The Ages of Man* in 1966 and in the mid-1970s for the ABC special *Eleanor and Franklin*.

A Westport summer resident in the '60s, he told a reporter at the time "the woes of the city disappear as soon as I get here." He noted the "slowing down" effect life in Westport had on him and his myriad activities.

DAVID SUSSKIND and *Open End* guest Harry Belafonte.

Phil Donahue

Trailblazing king of daytime talk TV, PHIL DONAHUE aired over 6,000 shows during a 29-year run with more than a million people in his studio audiences. Not afraid to take on controversial subjects, he often focused on the feminist movement and religious issues. The sympathetic-voiced Donahue stepped aside in 1996. But in 2002 he briefly returned to MSNBC with *Donahue*, a cable evening series that re-introduced him with the promotional line, "Be Thinkful. Donahue's Back."

Phil began his broadcast work at alma mater Notre Dame's commercial TV station. The talk show that would make him famous premiered in Dayton, Ohio, in 1967. This syndicated program won him many Emmys for Best Host. His *Donahue and Kids: Project Peacock* also received an Emmy for Outstanding Children's Program in 1981.

For many years Donahue shared a large waterfront estate in Westport with his wife, actress Marlo Thomas.

PHIL DONAHUE in lively debate on *Donahue*.

Rod Serling

Author of nearly 200 television plays, ROD SERLING (1924-1975) was the first video dramatist to have his works produced "live" a second time by popular demand. His network material appeared on early TV's programs, including *Kraft Theatre*, *Studio One* and *Playhouse 90*. An English lit major at Antioch College, he got a job with a Cincinnati TV station writing locally-shown dramas. As a freelancer in 1955, he wrote *Patterns*, winning his first Emmy. His script for *Requiem for a Heavyweight* won him another Emmy. Four more followed.

Serling became a television icon as creator, producer, and frequently author and narrator of *The Twilight Zone*. This anthology usually combined offbeat drama and science fiction. ("There is a fifth dimension...the dimension of imagination," he said to open each program and set the scene.) His *Night Gallery* series of supernatural vignettes, which he hosted, ran from 1970 to 1973. A games show fan, he was guest on many such shows, and in 1968-69 hosted *Liar's Club*.

As his earnings increased in the mid-1950s, Serling moved from Ohio to Westport, in order to be near the TV centers in Manhattan. The plots of several of his teleplays were set in Westport.

ROD SERLING, host on *Liar's Club*, with special guest, wife Carol Kramer (1968).

Martha Stewart

The multifaceted image of MARTHA STEWART became somewhat dimmed when unfavorable inside trader news overshadowed her omnimedia enterprises in 2002. Found guilty of lying about a stock sale of a biotechnology company and then serving a prison sentence briefly cast a cloud over her various TV series, including *Martha Stewart Living*, her leading syndicated show, which had won seven daytime Emmys.

Her career expanded from a catering business she started in Westport in the 1970s, not long after she purchased a fixer-upper farmhouse on Turkey Hill Road (that later became the model for the set of her TV program). Martha's big break came when Crown agreed to publish her book *Entertaining*. It was the first of her many bestselling volumes on style, cuisine and homemaking.

That book led to magazines, publishing, product catalogs, merchandising and television — where her personal lifestyle made her a media star, though she was occasionally "tarred and feathered" by the press.

Her own elaborate TV studio produced thousands of hours of programs. Her weekday one-hour series, known as *The Martha Stewart Show*, debuted in 2005, and was distributed by NBC Universal along with Martha's specials on fashion and design. Starting in 2010 these shows moved to the Hallmark Channel.

MARTHA STEWART, guest on NBC's *Today*, with Bryant Gumbel.

Sonny Fox

Kids growing up in the 1950s and '60s probably remember the pre-*Sesame Street* children's programs: *Let's Take a Trip, Just for Fun* and *Wonderama*. The Pied Piper of these daytime offerings was SONNY FOX of Weston. The entertainment factor was predominant but the educational quotient was more substantial than in almost any other children's program on commercial TV at that time.

Wonderama ended its run in 1967 — a program described by the *New York Times* as a blend of cultures, competitions, cartoons and commercials. "The most precious thing stations gave us was latitude to do anything we wanted, to pretty much leave us alone," Fox once remarked.

He started in broadcasting with radio's *Candid Mike* and *Voice of America* coverage of the Korean War. He soon moved into TV kiddies shows in St. Louis, then on to CBS New York. Leaving his role as host, he later turned full-time to executive producing.

At one point, in 1956, Sonny jumped into primetime as emcee of *The $64,000 Challenge*, a big-money spin-off of *The $64,000 Question*. It proved a disastrous move. In his own words: "People used to tune in to hear me ask the answers." A nervous, confused Fox often accepted wrong answers and added answers to questions! He did better as audience participation host of *On Your Mark* in 1961.

SONNY FOX's *Wonderama* and *Let's Take a Trip*, popular children's programs in the 1950s and '60s.

Jack Clark

JACK CLARK (1921-1988), best known as host of the popular syndicated game shows *Dealer's Choice* (1973-1975) and *The Cross-Wits* (1975-1980), began his broadcast career as a CBS staff announcer. An early assignment was introducing re-runs of dramas from various series for *Kodak Request Performance*, and announcing *The Big Surprise*, both in 1955.

Jack worked as announcer and substitute host on numerous audience participation shows: *To Tell the Truth, Password* and the original *Price Is Right*. He hosted the short-lived *100 Grand*, an attempt in 1963 by ABC to revive the "big money" game show killed by the quiz program scandals of the late 1950s. His last major assignment — "the voice behind the prizes" on top-rated *Wheel of Fortune* — ran from 1975 to 1988.

A onetime director and actor in San Francisco, Clark later commuted from Westport to Manhattan at a time when network game shows flourished on the East Coast.

JACK CLARK, host of *The Cross-Wits* (1975-1980).

Matt Gallant

Quick-witted, high-spirited Westport native MATT GALLANT rose from the ranks of NBC pages and commercial pitchmen to TV host/actor. Adding his talents to shows on MTV, ESPN, ABC, NBC and Fox, he leans toward comedy.

Matt enjoyed five seasons (2000-05) as host of the Animal Planet's series *The Planet's Funniest Animals*. Using home videos, documentary footage, news coverage, and more, the cable show offered Gallant's ongoing and humorous commentary as the clips rolled.

He also hosted ABC's reality show *American Inventor* and acted on *Brothers & Sisters*.

Matt has been a volunteer for the Make-A-Wish Foundation for over ten years, and holds an annual bowling event for charity in Los Angeles to raise both awareness and funds for the Foundation.

Broadcast Journalists

Philco 50-701 (1950).

Douglas Edwards

Network television's first nightly anchorman, DOUGLAS EDWARDS (1917-1990), started in video just before covering the 1948 Presidential conventions for CBS. *Douglas Edwards with the News* became a nightly news program at a time when few established radio reporters dared venture into TV.

Edwards had joined CBS during World War II after being an announcer on staff at radio stations in Atlanta and Detroit. A pioneer in electronic journalism, he first chaired the 15-minute newscast from a small studio in New York's Grand Central Station. One of the first to give eyewitness reports, he described the sinking of the Italian liner *Andrea Doria* in 1956. That year, he won a Peabody Award for best television news.

CBS also assigned him to host game shows (*Masquerade Party*) and dramatic anthologies (*Armstrong Circle Theatre*). Walter Cronkite succeeded him as nightly news anchor in the early 1960s. Edwards continued with a multitude of daily newscasts until his retirement after 45 years at a CBS mike.

A Conrail commuter, Edwards lived in Weston from 1949 to 1967.

DOUGLAS EDWARDS, checks material with Art Director Aaron Ehrlich, *CBS Television News*

Harry Reasoner

Described as "a star in the firmament of newscasters," HARRY REASONER (1923-1991) spent his long career at CBS and ABC. Wry wit and low-key delivery characterized his role as reporter and correspondent, beginning in 1956 with *CBS Morning News* and *CBS Reports*, plus various news specials. For *CBS News Hour* he won a 1968 Emmy for writing the documentary *What About Ronald Reagan?*

That year he joined the original news team of *60 Minutes*. He also served as CBS White House correspondent. Reasoner, however, had his eye on anchoring the CBS nightly newscast, but Walter Cronkite had nailed down that job. So in 1970 he moved to ABC News, where he co-anchored *The ABC Evening News*, first with Howard K. Smith and then Barbara Walters. While doing the weekly *Reasoner Report*, he received a 1974 Emmy as outstanding TV news broadcaster.

Reasoner returned to CBS in 1978 after ABC reshuffled its evening news show. He rejoined *60 Minutes*, which had become the most popular news journal on TV. He remained for 13 more seasons.

Named the most trusted network journalist in a 1982 survey, the veteran New York-based newsman lived in Weston, and later on Long Lots Road, Westport. "While I think of myself as a Midwesterner, actually I am more Connecticut than Midwest," he observed in the 1970s.

HARRY REASONER (left) and the *60 Minutes* team; Mike Wallace, Ed Bradley, Diane Sawyer, Morley Safer (1984).

John MacVane

Newspaper reporter JOHN MAC VANE (1912-1984) landed a job in Europe just as World War II broke out. Circumstances led to NBC radio work as foreign correspondent covering the London blitz, D-Day, the liberation of Paris, and the fall of Berlin. At war's end the authoritative, deep-voiced MacVane became chief NBC, later ABC, correspondent at the United Nations (until 1977).

By 1950 this post encompassed such TV coverage as *United or Not*, featuring interviews and discussions with guests from the UN. For NET he produced six 1960 documentaries on the new State of Alaska.

In retirement in the Greens Farms section of Westport he wrote his wartime memoirs, *On The Air in World War II*, including personal observations of Eisenhower, Churchill, De Gaulle and other Allied leaders.

JOHN MAC VANE, ABC News

John Siegenthaler

Contributing anchor at MSNBC Cable and anchor of weekend editions of *NBC Nightly News* (2000-07) JOHN SIEGENTHALER had been reporting news over TV since 1981, beginning in Seattle and Nashville. He joined NBC in 1996 as co-anchor of *Morning Line*, and soon served as special correspondent for *Dateline NBC* and hosted Dateline/Discovery Channel special reports.

Siegenthaler also anchored *MSNBC Investigates*, a documentary series covering such topics as bioterrorism, Afghanistan and Bin Laden's reign of terror. During election year 2000 he interviewed both Gore and Bush and reported on the political conventions.

A Weston resident, John has won two Emmys and the prestigious journalism awards, the Robert F. Kennedy Television News Prize, for a series of stories on the civil rights movement, and an American Bar Association award for his documentary on the death penalty. When NBC slashed its news division budget and cut jobs, Siegenthaler moved to the Associated Press until joining his family's public relations company in 2008.

Robert Hager

NBC News Correspondent for 35 years, ROBERT HAGER reported from Vietnam, Berlin, Moscow and elsewhere in Europe and the Middle East. Then, retired, he was a principal reporter during NBC's daylong "live" coverage of the terrorist attacks of 9/11, and is best known for aviation coverage from scenes of every major crash over 20 years.

A member of the Silver Circle honor society of journalists, Hager began as a broadcaster of minor league baseball in 1960 at station WBUY, Lexington, NC. He reported on state government and politics from Raleigh and Charlotte, and then moved on to news anchor for WRC-TV, Washington. Beginning in 1979, he was based in the Nation's Capital, and reputedly got more stories on *NBC Nightly News* than any other correspondent, year in and year out.

Both of Hager's parents were artists who moved to Westport in 1945 because it had a reputation as a colony of painters and illustrators. When he was assigned to NBC New York, he and his family chose Westport as their home from 1973 to 1979.

Pauline Frederick

Broadcasting's first woman network news analyst and diplomatic correspondent, PAULINE FREDERICK (1906-1990) covered the United Nations for more than 30 years. She broke into radio in 1939 while a newspaper journalist in Washington and into TV when assigned by ABC to cover the 1948 political conventions.

"I got into television quite unaware," she explained. "A notice had been posted that TV was coming and that anyone interested should sign up. I didn't sign up. I was finally getting some good radio assignments. But my news director said I'd be covering the Democratic Convention. I nearly fell off my chair." By 1976 she had become the first woman to moderate a Presidential debate, between Gerald Ford and Jimmy Carter.

Frederick interviewed guests from political, business and cultural life on *Pauline Frederick's Guestbook*, shortly after ABC inaugurated TV operations in 1948. She was featured on ABC's *All Star News* in 1952-53. She began a 21-year association with NBC in 1953, and the following year received a Peabody Award for contributing to international understanding. After mandatory retirement from NBC in 1974, she commented on foreign affairs for National Public Radio for another decade.

Frederick lived in a house overlooking Westport's Saugatuck River.

Eric Burns

ERIC BURNS, a media critic, author and journalist, began his career with NBC News, and had his own segment, "Cross Country" on the *Today* show. He also served as host of *Arts & Entertainment* on A&E.

While hosting *Fox News Watch*, reporting on the way the media covered the major stories of the day, Burns received an Emmy for media criticism.

Author of many books, he published in 2009 *All the News Unfit to Print: How Things Were...and How They Were Reported*. Earlier, his *The Spirits of America: A Social History of Alcohol* was named one of the best academic books of 2003 by the American Library Association.

Burns and his wife, Dianne Wildman, CT Cablevision director of editorial services, moved to Westport in the 1990s.

Dianne Wildman

Starting out as an *NBC Network News* correspondent in the early 1980s, DIANNE WILDMAN served in four bureaus: Burbank, Houston, New York and London. She also reported news and produced an Emmy-winning weekly public affairs program for KCET Los Angeles.

Prior to NBC, Wildman was a Peace Corps Volunteer in Micronesia. From 1993-96 she worked as Assistant Deputy US Trade Representative for Public Affairs in Washington. In 1997 she joined Cablevision as Director of Editorial Services in Connecticut. Her work on a series of editorials about Long Island Sound helped earn her a Save the Sound award. In 2003 she won an Outstanding Connecticut Women award, presented by Lt. Governor Jodi Rell.

Dianne is the wife of TV journalist and writer Eric Burns. "We arrived in Westport from LA in 1990, and then three years later were off to DC for the Clinton Administration. In '97 we returned and see no reason to keep moving on."

Gordon F. Joseloff

Award-winning journalist GORDON F. JOSELOFF reported from Moscow, Tokyo and other world capitals for CBS News and UPI for over two decades. He started at CBS as a writer for Walter Cronkite and Dan Rather, and went on to cover some of the world's major stories of the late 1970s and 1980s — everything from presidential summits and economic conferences to disasters, riots and revolutions. He also coordinated special projects for CBS News in New York and helped to organize its coverage of the 1991 Gulf War.

Joseloff has been honored by the Writers Guild of America for news writing. He founded and became editor-in-chief and publisher of *WestportNow*, an award-winning local news and information website.

He is very active in the community, having served as a volunteer fireman and moderator on the Westport Representative Town Meeting for ten years. He was elected Westport's First Selectman in 2005, and reelected later.

Joseloff began his journalism career as a teen-age reporter for the now-defunct local newspaper, *Westport Town Crier*.

GORDON JOSELOFF reports from Gdansk, Poland, on shipyard strikes for CBS News.

Sports

Sony KV-1512 (1977).

Brent Musburger

In an age of mass media coverage, BRENT MUSBURGER has been called a "generalist" in his field thanks to his broad knowledge of many sports. Sportscaster and journalist-type announcer, Brent trained at Northwestern School of Journalism then worked as a sportswriter for the *Chicago American*. In 1968 Chicago's CBS radio station switched to an all-news format and needed sportscasters for the Mexico City Olympics. He was hired.

Musburger moved over to CBS-TV in 1974, doing *NBA Basketball* and *NFL Today*. He also hosted *NCAA Today, Saturday/Sports Sunday* and *Sports Time*. In the 1990s he joined ABC as sports announcer. That network's association with ESPN allowed Brent to have two venues to broadcast from. He is regarded as the first to apply the term "March Madness" to the annual NCAA Basketball tourney.

A frequent Emmy nominee, the low-keyed Brent chose Weston as home where he values his privacy. "You have to get away from the arena where we're heavily identified," he once remarked, "and this is where I get away from it."

BRENT MUSBURGER chats with tug-of-war competitors on *World's Strongest Men* series (1977).

Sal Marchiano

A sportscaster for major networks for over 40 years, SAL MARCHIANO retired as sports director and anchor for WPIX *Channel 11 News at Ten* in 2008.

He began in radio while a Fordham undergrad, and then joined CBS, before moving on to ABC's *Eyewitness News* and *Wide World of Sports*.

Marchiano was an original cast member of ESPN in 1979, anchoring *Sportscenter* and *Sportsforum*, and calling the channel's boxing matches. To meet Connecticut-based ESPN's schedule, he moved to Westport, his home for 20+ years. "I used to take rides up there on weekends and always loved the place." The Brooklyn native, who worked at WNBC-TV before joining Channel 11 in 1994, won an Emmy for his sportscasting on *News at Ten*.

Called the voice of New York sports — be it baseball, boxing or football — he wrote of four decades in broadcasting in his memoir, *In My Rearview Mirror*.

SAL MARCHIANO interviews NFL's Pete Rozelle (1981).

Bob Costas

NBC sportscaster and Olympic Games anchor since 1992, BOB COSTAS is liable to pop up on TV programs other than those covering sports. At times provokingly outspoken, he's been a correspondent for *Dateline NBC* and *Now with Tom Brokaw and Katie Couric.* From 1988 to 1994 he hosted *Later*, a celebrity interview show. It received a 1994 Emmy for outstanding informational special. Costas appears often on *Late Night with David Letterman.* And he even was heard as a caller to *Frasier's* program (asking a complicated basketball question).

Bob joined NBC Sports in 1980, and soon handled *Game of the Week* telecasts, especially baseball, his favorite sport. He combined talk about sports, news and entertainment on HBO's late-night series *On the Record with Bob Costas.* He is a contributor to MLB Network's *Studio 42.*

Recipient of numerous National Sportscaster of the Year awards, Costas studied as a communications major at Syracuse, but left to do *Spirits of St. Louis* play-by-play at KMOX radio.

A personal influence has been legendary sports broadcaster, fellow Westporter Jim McKay.

BOB COSTAS and Tony Kubek, NBC's *Game of the Week* baseball coverage.

Jim Nantz

Young JIM NANTZ believed in his dream. He wanted to call sports on television. But not for just any network. It had to be CBS. Before graduating from college in Houston, he gained experience by working at a small radio station and anchoring on a local CBS TV channel.

The network hired him in 1985 to host a college football show. He soon joined the CBS golf coverage team, and then became play-by-play announcer for football. In 1990 he added college basketball. Nantz has called play-by-play on more network broadcasts of NCAA Final Four and championships than any other announcer in the tournament's history. In 2002 Nantz received the Curt Gowdy Award, given to members of the media who make an outstanding contribution to basketball.

He has hosted *The Super Bowl Today*, CBS coverage of the Olympics and *College Football Today*.

"I live in Westport because as a boy I wrote a letter to Jim McKay and Win Elliot and they wrote me back," he notes. "When I was hired by CBS, there was no question I wanted to live in the same town where they raised their families."

JIM NANTZ, CBS sportscaster, with Tiger Woods.

Jim McKay

TV commentator or host at 12 Olympics, including the 2002 Winter Games for NBC, JIM MCKAY (1921-2008) became in 1968 the first sports broadcaster to win an Emmy Award. Since then he won a dozen more. He covered more than 100 different sports in 40 countries — many for ABC's *Wide World of Sports*. McKay was that program's host on its very first day in 1961.

Regarded as the Dean of Sports Commentators, he has been honored with a Peabody Award and the George Polk Memorial Award for Journalism. In 1995 he was installed in the Television Academy Hall of Fame.

McKay debuted on TV at WMAR Baltimore in 1947. In the 1950s, for the CBS courtroom drama *The Verdict is Yours*, McKay played the role of court reporter, and on that network's discussion series, *Youth Takes a Stand*, he acted as moderator.

For many years he lived in Westport. In 2002 he returned to receive the first Westport/Weston YMCA's "Spirit, Mind and Body Lifetime Achievement Award."

JIM McKAY published his memoirs in 1973.

Frank Deford

Versatile writer FRANK DEFORD came to broadcasting in the 1980s after many years as senior contributing writer at *Sports Illustrated*. A commentator on National Public Radio, CNN and ESPN, he worked as features correspondent for *NFL Today* and the Seoul Olympics at NBC. Deford won a 1988 Emmy for writing during those Olympics — specifically for a piece on the families of the Israeli athletes slain at the '72 games.

Since 1995 he is the senior correspondent on *Real Sports with Bryant Gumbel*, an HBO show. He has also narrated documentaries on PBS and the History Channel. He won a Peabody Award recently for writing the HBO presentation *Dare To Compete*, a history of female athletes. A member of the Hall of Fame of the National Association of Sportscasters & Sportswriters, he is the author of 16 books, including the novels *An American Summer* and *Everybody's All-American*. Several of his books and screenplays have also been filmed.

Deford resides in Greens Farms, Westport, and contributes a popular weekly sports column to the *Westport News*. In 2010, he received the Westport Arts Award for Literature.

FRANK DEFORD, Bryant Gumbel, *Real Sports* for HBO.

Sitcoms Come to Westport

Motorola 9T1 with antenna (1949).

Three comedy series from the heyday of television sitcoms claimed Westport as their locale, although none of them were ever filmed on location in town.

I Love Lucy

Lucy (Lucille Ball) and Ricky Ricardo (Desi Arnaz) moved from Manhattan, along with their city neighbors, Fred and Ethel Mertz (William Frawley and Vivian Vance), in the final ten months of the *I Love Lucy* half-hour series in 1957.

In one memorable episode Lucy chairs the Yankee Doodle Day committee for the Historical Society, but she accidentally destroys Westport's landmark Minuteman statue at its unveiling. She then tries to stand in for the shattered memorial with hilarious results.

One of the show's writers, Bob Weiskopf, drew upon his own experience moving from New York to Westport as he helped craft these zany "country neighborhood" scripts for the Ricardos and the Mertzs.

Bewitched

This show also claimed Westport as its fictional home. In fact, one of the first proposed names for the series was *The Witch of Westport*. In the show's second episode in 1964, the pretty young witch Samantha (Elizabeth Montgomery) and her mortal ad agency husband Darrin (Dick York) moved to a fictitious Westport address, 1164 Morning Glory Circle. The couple's "house" was actually built on the Warner Brothers back-lot in Burbank, California.

This ABC series gathered a superb supporting cast during its eight-year run: Agnes Moorehead, Mable Albertson, Maurice Evans, Alice Ghostley, Marion Lorne, and such guest stars as Imogene Coca as a tooth fairy and Paul Lynde as a warlock.

My World and Welcome to It

This sitcom based on the life and works of James Thurber, who spent weekends and vacations in Westport, pivoted around the fictional writer-cartoonist John Monroe. The lead character with an overly active imagination (played by William Windom) lives in Westport and commutes to New York City for his job with a magazine called *The Manhattanite*. His fears as well as his dream world give the episodes an aspect of fantasy, underscored by an animated Thurber-like home.

Index

Adams, Mason 66, 67
Akins, Claude 83
Albert, Eddie 120, 121
Albertson, Mabel 103, 118, 119
Alexander, Rod 166, 167
Allen, Woody 48, 160
Ames, Nancy 102, 113
Ames, Elinor 29
Anderson, Kevin 78
Andrews, Dana 44, 45
Aniston, Jennifer 115
Arkin Alan 43, 46, 47
Arkin, Adam 46, 106
Arnaz, Desi 222
Asner, Ed 67
Bader, Diedrich 96, 97
Ball, Lucille 222
Banks, Joan 64, 81
Bauer, Charita 135
Baxter, Anne 36
Belafonte, Harry 177
Bessell, Ted 114
Bethune, Zina 157
Bixby, Bill 68
Black, Michael Ian 125
Black, Ed 33

Blondell, Joan 104, 105
Bradley, Ed 193
Brennan, Walter 104
Brent, Romney 22
Bridges, Lloyd 106
Bryce, Ed 25, 134, 135
Bryce, Scott 136, 137
Bryce, Dorothy 24, 25, 135
Burns, Eric 202, 203
Caesar, Sid 122, 123, 166
Calvert, James 160
Camargo, Ralph 150, 151
Carey-Lamm, Susan 139
Carter, Jack 110
Cassidy, Shaun 72
Chapman Lisa 152
Clark, Jack 186, 187
Coca, Imogene 122, 123, 166
Cole, Jack 166, 167
Coleman, Dabney 160
Collin, Joan 57
Connell, John 141
Connor, Whit 84, 85, 154, 156, 157
Conroy, Kevin 138, 139
Converse, Frank 82, 83
Cosby, Bill 109

Costas, Bob 212, 213
Cronkite, Walter 92, 191, 192, 204
Dabney, Augusta 140, 141
Danza, Tony 101
Darrid, Bill 58
Davis, Bette 36, 37
Day, Doris 114
Deford, Frank 218, 219
DeLong, Tom 25, 134, 135
Dennis, Patrick 50
Denver, Bob 51
DeVito, Danny 101
Donahue, Phil 115, 178, 179
Dorne, Albert 202, 203
Douglas, Diana 58, 59, 63
Douglas, Michael 58, 59, 62, 63
Douglas, Kirk 58, 59, 63
Edwards, Douglas 13, 190, 191
Ehrlich, Aaron 191
Elliot, Win 28, 29, 215
Englund, Patricia 102, 103, 118
Evans, Monica 53
Farrow, Mia 48, 49
Ferrante, Frank 94, 96
Flynn, Errol 144
Fonda, Henry 122
Ford, Faith 42, 136
Forster, Robert 104
Forsythe, John 73
Fox, Sonny 184, 185
Frawley, William 222
Frederick, Pauline 200, 201
Frost, David 102
Furness, Betty 105
Gabor, Eva 120, 121

Gallant Matt 188
Garner, James 68
Garroway, Dave 24
Gibb, Cindy 100, 160
Gorshin, Frank 126, 127
Grant, David M. 78
Gray, Coleen 45
Green, Adolph 112
Green, Johnny 23
Greene, Lorne 57
Groh, David 130, 131
Gumbel, Bryant 183, 218, 219
Hager, Robert 198
Haines Larry 142, 143
Hale, Jr. Alan 51
Hamilton, Neil 74
Hanson, O.B 16, 17
Harper, Ron 77
Harper, Valerie 130, 131
Harris, Rosemary 31
Harrison, Gregory 108
Hartley, Mariette 68, 69
Havoc, June 84, 85, 156, 160
Hayden, Michael 80
Heath, Andrew 153
Henner, Marilu 101
Hirsch, Judd 101
Hobbs, Peter 155
Holloway, Freda 141
Hopkins, John 42
Houseman, John 59
Hudson, Rock 116
Imus, Don 174, 175
Irwin, Carlotta 170
Jenner, Bruce 73

INDEX

Joseloff, Gordon 204, 205
Kahn, Madeline 108, 109
Kalember, Patricia 88, 89
Kane, Carol 101
Kennedy, George 106
Kenney-Silver, Kerri 124
Kenney, Larry 124
Keppler, Victor 20, 21
Kiley, Richard 39
Kitt, Eartha 162, 163
Klugman, Jack 74, 75, 106, 110, 111
Knight, Shirley 42, 43
Kramer, Carol 181
Kubek, Tony 213
Kurtz, Swoosie 89
Lancaster, Burt 142
Lang, Stephen 41
Lawrence, Gertrude 54, 55
Le Gallienne, Eva 30, 31, 140, 166
Lee, Gypsy Rose 84
Lennon, Thomas 124, 125
Leonard, Bill 26, 27
Lynn, Bambi 166, 167
Lloyd, Christopher 100, 101
Lodge, John 32, 33
Lodge, Francesca 33
Louise, Tina 50, 51
Lovejoy, Frank 64, 65, 81
MacVane, John 194
Malden, Karl 62, 63
Malkovich, John 40, 41
Marchand, Nancy 67
Marchiano, Sal 210, 211
Marcus, Kipp 128, 129
Marcus, Adam 128

Marshall, E.G. 74
Martin, Pamela Sue 72, 73
Martin, Dick 110
Massey, Raymond 30
Matheson, Tim 88
Mayehoff, Eddie 118
Maynard, Diana 149
McGavin, Darren 70, 71
McKay, Jim 213, 215, 216, 217
McMahon, Ed 132
Melton James 164, 165
Montgomery, Elizabeth 224
Moore, Mary Tyler 68, 110, 114
Morris, Howard 123
Mulligan, Richard 68
Musburger, Brent 208, 209
Nantz, Jim 214, 215
Naughton, James 76, 77
Newman, Phyllis 102, 112, 113
Newman, Paul 38, 76, 77, 86, 87
Nobel, James 25
O'Neal, Ryan 49
O'Sullivan, Maureen 48
Orenstein, Bernie 107
Phillips, Julianne 89
Plummer, Christopher 56, 57
Plummer, Amanda 57
Porter, Alisan 132
Powell, Norman 105
Prince, William 140, 141
Rabb, Ellis 31
Rae, Melba 143
Randall, Tony 75, 111
Rashad, Phylicia 109
Rather, Dan 204

Rayburn, Gene 110
Raye, Martha 116, 117, 168
Reagan, Ronald 84, 144, 192
Reasoner, Harry 192, 193
Reed, Carol 33
Reid, Elliot 102
Reilly, Charles Nelson 110
Reiner, Fritz 170, 171
Reiner, Carl 123
Rhoades, Barbara 106
Roberts, Roy 119
Rogers, Dulcy 96, 97
Rogers, David 92, 93, 94, 96
Rogers, Amanda 94, 95, 96
Rowlands, Gena 37
Rozelle, Pete 211
Runyeon, Frank 146, 147
Ryan, Meg 136, 146, 147
Safer, Morley 193
Saint, Eva Marie 86, 87
Sarnoff, David 17
Sawyer, Diane 193
Scacheri, Mabel 20
Scott, George C. 91, 108
Sedaka, Neil 168, 169
Serling, Rod 180, 181
Shapiro, Kitt 162
Shaw, George B. 54
Shelley, Carole 52, 53
Siegenthaler, John 196, 197
Silvers, Phil 24
Sinatra, Frank 86, 87
Smith, Howard K. 192
Somers, Brett 110, 111
Sothern, Ann 81

Spaeth, Sigmund 22, 23
Stevenson, Parker 72
Stewart, Martha 182, 183
Stoddard, Haila 154, 155, 156
Streep, Meryl 76, 137
Stuart, Mary 30, 143, 144, 145
Suiter, Bobra 158
Susskind, David 176. 177
Tayback, Vic 117
Thomas, Marlo 114, 115, 118, 179
Thomas, Danny 115
Thurber, James 154, 226
Tomlin, Lily 150
Vance, Vivian 222
Wagner, Robert 36
Wallace, Mike 193
Walters, Barbara 192
Ward, Sela 89
Warden, Jack 66
Watson, Douglas 151
Wayne, David 54, 55, 168
Weiskopf, Bob 222
Weitz, Bruce 60, 61
West, Martin 148, 149
White, Michael Jai 90, 91
White, Betty 110
Whiting, Margaret & Barbara 118
Wildman, Dianne 202, 203
Wilson, Mary 81
Windom, William 226
Woods, Tiger 215
Woods, Wally 25
Woodward, Joanne 38, 39, 76, 87
Wyndham, Victoria 150, 151
York, Dick 224

Bibliography

DeLong, T.A. *Stars in Our Eyes: Luminaries of Stage and Screen At Home in Westport and Weston, CT.* Westport Historical Society, Westport, Connecticut, 2000

Goldstein, Norm. *The History of Television.* Portland House, New York, 1991

Grebow, Marion with Curran, Dorothy. *River of Names: An Historical Tile Mural at the Westport Public Library.* Westport Library Association, Westport, Connecticut, 2001.

Klein, Woody. *Westport Connecticut: The Story of a New England Town's Rise to Prominence.* Greenwood Press, Westport, Connecticut, 2000.

Potts, Eve. *Westport, A Special Place.* Westport Historical Society, Westport, Connecticut, 1985.

About the Author

THOMAS A. DELONG is the award-winning biographer and author of many books about radio and television. Among these are:

Madame Chiang Kai-shek and Miss Emma Mills: China's First Lady and her American Friend (2007)

John Davis Lodge: A Life in Three Acts — Actor, Politician, Diplomat (2001)

Stars In Our Eyes: Luminaries of Stage and Screen at Home in Westport and Weston in the 20th Century (2000)

Radio Stars (1996)

Frank Munn – The Golden Voice of Radio (1994)

Quiz Craze: America's Infatuation with Game Shows (1991)

POPS: Paul Whiteman, King of Jazz (1983)

The Mighty Music Box – The Golden Age of Radio (1980)

He has written feature articles for *Films in Review, New York Times, FM Guide, Los Angeles Times, Stamford Advocate, Classic Images, Connecticut Post* and *Westport Magazine.*

Tom died in July 2010, having completed the draft of this, his final volume.

Bear Manor Media

Classic Cinema.
Timeless TV.
Retro Radio.

WWW.BEARMANORMEDIA.COM

www.ingramcontent.com/pod-product-compliance
Lightning Source LLC
Chambersburg PA
CBHW071433150426
43191CB00008B/1119